THE WELLSPRING OF WORSHIP

JEAN CORBON

THE WELLSPRING
OF
WORSHIP

Translated by Matthew J. O'Connell

IGNATIUS PRESS   SAN FRANCISCO

Original French edition *Liturgie de Source* published by
Les Editions Du Cerf, Paris. © 1980 by Les Editions Du Cerf.
First English edition © 1988 by
The Missionary Society of St. Paul the Apostle

Cover art:
Icon of the Old Testament Trinity, ca. 1410.
Rublev, Andrei (1360–c. 1430)
Tretyakov Gallery, Moscow, Russia
© Scala / Art Resource, New York

Cover design by Roxanne Mei Lum

Second edition published in 2005 by Ignatius Press
Published with permission of Les Editions Du Cerf
This edition published by Ignatius Press, San Francisco
ISBN 978-1-58617-022-6
Library of Congress Control Number 2004114954
Printed in the United States of America ∞

CONTENTS

PART ONE
The Mystery of the Liturgy

PART TWO
The Liturgy Celebrated

FOREWORD TO THE ENGLISH EDITION

Everything that can be identified as a peculiarly Christian truth is, in one way or another, a derivative of the one central truth that man was created in order to live forever in personal communion with the Holy Trinity. The explicit revelation of the transcendent goal of man's existence was given in and through the history of Jesus of Nazareth and the history of the special mission of the Holy Spirit that followed upon his death, Resurrection, and glorification. With the sending of the Spirit from the Father through the risen Lord to bind believers to the beloved Son, and so bring them into personal communion with the Father of all, the ecclesial body of Christ was born.

The Church of Jesus Christ is the concrete place in history where this trinitarian mystery is explicitly proclaimed and accepted, where the Father's offer of self-communication through his only Son and his Holy Spirit finds a free response of praise and thanksgiving. This mystery is represented and shared in a festive way in the liturgy of the Church; it is continually offered and accepted in all the dimensions of the daily life of faith.

When one begins to think about this deepest meaning of the liturgy of the Church, it becomes clear what the goal of a theology of liturgy should be. A comprehensive explanation of the meaning of the liturgy must take the path that leads back to the life work of the triune God. It must be shown how Christian liturgy in general, and the chief liturgical-sacramental celebrations of the Church, derive from and are ordered to the deepest and proper mystery of Christian faith: the self-communication of the triune God in a history of salvation that is the first fruits of the trinitarian-heavenly liturgy, already in progress since the Ascension of Jesus Christ, and the ascension of those who have died in the Lord.

But how is one to achieve this goal? As a matter of fact, an explicit trinitarian theology of the liturgy has not been handed down to us in the theological traditions of the Eastern and Western Church. Nowadays the ideas of theology of the liturgy as theology of the Trinity are in the air. But there have been very few attempts to work out a systematic approach to this subject. Since there is a scarcity of models that might serve as the basis for further reflection, this project represents a real challenge. In recent time, some theologians have introduced a theology of the Trinity into their systematic reflection on the liturgy and sacraments. But generally the references to the Trinity serve only as a helpful means of pointing out what must be included in a comprehensive theology of liturgy.

This work of Jean Corbon is an exception. He has contributed an attractive presentation of the theology of liturgy, inspired by the witness of Scripture and patristic sources of the Syriac and Greek traditions. While there exist many similarities with modern contributions to the understanding of the liturgy, it would be a mistake to characterize this book as nothing more than a continuation of the literature that focused on the christological dimension of the liturgical event: the active presence of Jesus Christ and his saving mysteries. This work cannot even be described as unfolding the implications of the personal mission of the Holy Spirit for a better understanding of the active role of the Spirit in the liturgy, in continuity with traditional Eastern theology and benefiting from the insights of some modern Western Catholic theologians.

Rather, the central intuition of Corbon is *trinitarian* and the insights derived from this intuition show the way to a very promising new direction for liturgical theology as a whole, the classical Scholastic treatise on principles of sacramental theology, and the traditional seven sacraments. The thoughtful reader, especially one standing in the Western tradition, will find unexpected riches beneath these unpretentious sections: "The Mystery of the Liturgy", "The Liturgy Celebrated", and "The Liturgy Lived".

Edward J. Kilmartin, S.J.
Professor, Pontifical Oriental Institute, Italy

FOREWORD TO THE FRENCH EDITION

This book begins with a short list of liturgical terms. Father Corbon is right to provide it; the fact, however, that we need it is certainly no great compliment to us Western Christians. The truth is that we are no longer able to understand the language commonly spoken among Christians of the early centuries. Instead, we have for many centuries circled round and round in the confines of our very rational and very juridical Latin form of Christianity.

Our Eastern brothers and sisters attach greater importance than we do to the liturgy. We can imagine, therefore, how happy they were to see Vatican II begin its work with a consideration of the liturgy.

Liturgical reform has been under way in the Latin Church since before the Council. But, as Father Corbon observes, the leaders of the liturgical renewal have sometimes focused their attention solely on the modalities of celebration and have not helped us truly to enter into the liturgical mystery.

The present essay on the mystery of the liturgy will make it possible for the faithful of our various Churches to get back to the "source", the wellspring. It was in light of the "mystery" that the New Testament, the early Church, and the Church of the Fathers approached everything. This must once again become our approach, under the inspiration of Vatican II, where everything was renewed in terms of it.

Because the liturgy is a "source", it unfolds in all dimensions of the mystery and assumes, saves, and divinizes all that is human, from the most deeply personal to the most openly communal. And this "energy" of the river of life, which in the liturgy becomes a "synergy" of the Spirit and the Church, flows precisely through the "place" and "moment" constituted by our celebrations.

An emphasis on the unity of liturgy and life will characterize the dialogue on this theme that has now begun in the Mixed Catholic-Orthodox Commission for Theological Dialogue, the establishment of which John Paul II and the Ecumenical Patriarch Demetrios announced at their meeting on November 30, 1979.

Father Corbon's book may come as a surprise to some. When the two poles in the soul of the undivided Church begin their mutual rediscovery, neither can fail to be surprised by the other. *The Wellspring of Worship*, which is located at the ever-present origination point of the undivided tradition, will inevitably stir that kind of wonder. The approach taken here to the liturgy makes the mystery its starting point; it does not neglect the conditions needed for concrete liturgy, but it does illumine them from within, thus transfiguring them. Ever since the first Catholic-Orthodox meeting that ended with the lifting of excommunications (December 7, 1965), this approach based on the mystery is the thing that the Catholic participants have found most striking in their Orthodox brethren.

The purpose of the present book is to help deepen this rediscovery through an ecclesial experience of the liturgy. Our thanks to Father Corbon for guiding us on this return to the source.

Cardinal Roger Etchegaray

PREFACE

In the liturgical springtime that most of the churches are experiencing today, there is one question that young people, adults, educators, and even pastors cannot evade: Do our celebrations, lively though they may be, change the lives of Christians? Where is the vital link—or, possibly, the divorce—between liturgy and life? The question is one of the most serious a mature Christian can ask. It is no less serious for the communion of churches, since in the springtime of which I speak the mystery of the liturgy seems to be the basis for the unity that is taking shape.

My purpose in this book is to help readers rediscover the unity of liturgy and life in Christ and not be satisfied with the mere parallelism or even divergence they mistakenly think exists between the two. We will be engaged less in a learned inquiry than in a prayerful discovery of the wellspring of worship. Our guide will be the experience of the Church: an experience that is at once liturgical and spiritual, personal, and communal and is illumined by the Bible and the Fathers.

This means that the book is also ecumenical in its inspiration. Each ecclesial tradition will be able to recognize itself in the common, undivided tradition. There may be more frequent references to the Byzantine tradition, but I have tried to remain on the original level at which the liturgies of both East and West embody the Christian liturgy.[1]

---

[1] In an earlier work, *L'Eglise des Arabes* (Paris: Cerf, 1977), I promised to develop some aspects of the theology by which the Antiochene Churches still live. The present book is a first essay along these lines.

A symbol: the river of life (Rev 22:1f.) will serve to light the way for our gradual discovery. I ask the readers to let themselves be carried along by this river's slow but deep-running current. Each chapter, at times more contemplative, at times more didactic, will help reveal the mystery of the source; the wellspring is ever the same, but the living water that flows from it is ever new.

A LITURGICAL VOCABULARY

In this book, in which we shall be contemplating the mystery of the liturgy from within, the reader will rarely find the learned terminology proper to formal theology or the human sciences. On the other hand, biblical revelation as actualized in the spiritual experience of the early Church could not but employ a new vocabulary to express the newness found in the liturgy. These new words cannot be translated without distortion into our modern languages, which are based more on objects than on the mystery and are more descriptive than symbolical. The old wineskins of a rational vocabulary cannot hold and contain the new realities suggested by such words as Christ, Holy Spirit, Gospel, Pentecost, Church, baptism, and Eucharist.

We must therefore acquaint ourselves with certain biblical and patristic words if we are to participate in the mystery that they reveal. The liturgical renewal has already made most of them familiar to us. I give here a list of the most important and frequently occurring ones, even though I explain them again in the text when they appear for the first time. Readers should not hesitate to let these words fill and permeate them, for, while the Gospel reveals the kingdom to us in parables, the liturgy gives us an experience of it in symbols.

Agape: "love". The last and most beautiful name for God in the New Testament: "God is agape" (1 Jn 4:8, 16). Agape is love that springs from goodness, from pure grace, without any nonvolitional cause; it is life giving; it renders its object lovable and gives it a participation in the communion that is the Blessed Trinity. This is why agape is the mystery at the heart of the Church and why the Eucharist, which is the liturgical reality of the Church, is likewise called agape.

Anamnesis: "reminder, remembrance". In the liturgical celebration the Church remembers all the saving events that God brought about in history and that had their climax and fulfillment in the Cross and Resurrection of Christ. But the paschal event, which occurred only once in history, is contemporary with each moment of our lives, for now that Christ is risen, he has broken through the wall of mortal time. The liturgy is thus a "memorial" of an utterly new kind. We do the remembering, but the reality remembered is no longer in the past but is here: the Church's memory becomes a presence. From this we can gauge the unsurpassed realism of the event that is the liturgy.

Anaphora: "a carrying on high". Every liturgical celebration is an anaphora because it shares in the present movement of the Lord's Ascension (see chapter 4). More precisely, the anaphora is the central movement of the Eucharist (the "eucharistic prayer" of the Latin liturgy) and consists of the thanksgiving, the anamnesis, the epiclesis, and the intercessions.

Doxology: simultaneously "singing of the glory" of God and "profession of the faith" of the Church. "God's glory is man fully alive", but "the glory of man is God" (Saint Irenaeus of Lyons). The economy of human salvation becomes doxology in the liturgy.

Economy: see Eph 3:9. The economy is more than simply the "history of salvation"; it is the dispensation, or wise arrangement by stages, whereby the mystery that is Christ

is brought to fulfillment. From Pentecost on, the economy has become liturgy because we are in the stage of
response and of the synergy (see further on) of Spirit
and Church.

Energy: this word, which says more than "action" or "operation", has to do with life-giving power; in our context
it is the life-giving power of the living God and more
particularly that of the Holy Spirit. When the energy of
man is brought into play by the Spirit and linked to the
energy of God, there is a "synergy" (see below). The
liturgy is essentially a synergy of the Spirit and the Church
(see chapter 8).

Epiclesis: "calling down upon". It is an "invocation"
addressed to the Father that he would send his Spirit on
the Church's offering so that this may be changed into
the Body of Christ. The epiclesis is the central moment
in every sacramental anaphora; it is that which gives the
Christian liturgy its new and distinct efficacy. Ordained
ministers are there primarily to serve the epiclesis, for
they are servants of the Spirit, who acts with power. "Epiclesis" is a very important word throughout this book.
The epiclesis is the vehicle of the mightiest synergy of
God and men, both in the celebration and in the living
out of the liturgy.

Kenosis: see Phil 2:7. The noun is derived from the verb
"he emptied himself" or "annihilated himself" that is
used in this passage. The Son remains God when he
becomes incarnate, but he divests himself of his glory
to the point of being "unrecognizable" (see Is 53:2–3).
Kenosis is the properly divine way of loving: becoming
man without reservation and without calling for recognition or compelling it. Kenosis refers first to the self-
emptying of the Word in the Incarnation, but this is

completed in the self-emptying of the Spirit in the Church, while it also reveals the self-emptying of the living God in creation. The mystery of the Covenant stands under the sign of kenosis, for the more far-reaching the covenant, the more complete the union. Our divinization comes through the meeting of the kenosis of God with the kenosis of man; the fundamental requirement of the Gospel can therefore be stated as follows: we shall be one with Christ to the extent that we "lose" ourselves for him. See also chapter I, note 5.

Koinonia: a word often used in the writings of Saint Paul and Saint John. It means the "communion" of the Holy Spirit, who unites us to the Father through Christ. It is a participation in the divine life. The Church is essentially a koinonia. See also agape.

Mystagogy: "action of leading into the mystery" or "action by which the mystery leads us". See chapter 10, note 12.

Synergy: along with epiclesis, one of the key words of this book. See chapter 2, note 4, and chapter 8, note 1. Literally: "joint activity", combined energies. This classical term of the Fathers attempts to express what is novel in the union of God and man in Christ and, more specifically, what is novel in the energy of the Holy Spirit that permeates the energy of men and conforms them to Christ. The full realism of the liturgy and of our divinization has its source in this synergy. See also energy, economy, epiclesis, and kenosis.

Time: the familiar word, but transfigured by biblical revelation and liturgical experience. The economy of salvation includes several "times": the beginning of time; the course or unfolding of time (beginning with the promise); the fullness of time (see Gal 4:4); the last times (or "eschatological" times), which are the time of the Church and the liturgy; and, finally, the consummation or fulfillment of time (the Second Coming of the Lord). The language of the Bible also distinguishes "decisive moments" (*kairoi*) within the time of the economy; see chapter 4, note 3. On the new time begun by the Resurrection of Christ and its sacramental celebration, see chapter 13.

Beside the Well

Men thirst and look for water wherever they think they will find it. As they wander without any horizon in sight and no way of escape, they dig a well each time they pitch their tent. The wonderful thing is that the history of their salvation always begins with the digging of a well. "We find the patriarchs constantly digging wells." [1] We ourselves are these patriarchs, traversing a promised land as strangers in our own inheritance. Beside their wells they also build altars to their gods: their religion, their ideology, their money, their power. Men are thirsty: How could they fail to dig where they think they may find water?

Even the denials that spring up from our atheistic unconsciousness betray our nostalgia. "They say that they thirst not; they say that this is not a well, that this is not water. They say that this is not a well of water as they have imagined it to be, and they say there is no water." [2] But these same men, so sure of themselves, cannot but continue to be still expectant, for to stop thirsting would mean they were already sunk in the sleep of death.

Nor does he sleep who placed in the human soul both the thirst and the expectation. Indeed, he is the first to thirst and to set out in search of us, to the point of joining us beside our pathetic wells. "Start with these wells, traverse the Scriptures

[1] Origen, *Homilies on Genesis* 13.
[2] Paul Claudel, *The Humiliation of the Father*, act II, sc. 2, in *Three Plays*, trans. J. Heard (Boston, 1945), 185.

in search of wells, and reach the Gospels. There you will find
the well beside which our Savior was resting, wearied by his
journey, when a Samaritan woman came to draw water from
it." [3]

It is beside the well that he waits for us. The conversation
always leads, by way of our evasions and hostilities, to the
unavoidable question of the temple or place of encounter
between God and man and of water and the thirst for it.
"Neither on this mountain nor in Jerusalem": Where, then,
is the place of the new liturgy, the infinitely rich place where
life rediscovers its source?

For some the only wells in question are their own. The
fountain of living water? "They have abandoned . . . the fountain of living water and dug water-tanks for themselves,
cracked water-tanks that hold no water" (Jer 2:13). Thus,
for the activists inspired by love, the Gospel is action and
must be taken seriously: the Lazarus of the parable is at our
doors; why then should they waste time at the symbolic fes-
tival of the evil rich? Then there are the purists of class struggle: they refuse to enter because it would be a lie for them to
share the agape with the sinners who oppress the poor outside the temple. Finally, there are the solitary mystics, averse
to all forms of celebration: in their view Christ transcended
this whole business with his ideal of "worship in spirit and
truth"; angels are not interested in fountains.

Beside the well Christ also awaits the Samaritan women
of the New Covenant. These realize that the spring of water
exists, and they are looking for it, but they have forgotten
that it wells up in him who asks them for a drink. The fountain has become a mirage. In this group we find the manu-
facturers of liturgies and the tireless composers; they are

[3] Origen, *Homilies on Numbers* 12.

fascinated by life and anxious for authenticity, and therefore on each occasion they invent anew the celebration of their life. Then too there are the lovers of the archaic and the purists who focus on form: the way to the fountain is enough for them, because for centuries it has guided believers. Also on this path, where security is the main concern, we find those who have fled from the vale of tears; they forget real life for a moment and immerse themselves in a heavenly liturgy—but what kind of heavenly liturgy is it?

This leaves these—undoubtedly the majority of the faithful—who do not ask so many questions and pass in a very simple way from Sabbath to Resurrection. Their attachment to Sunday and its paschal Eucharist is really astounding when we realize that they are unable to say why they are attached. It is precisely this "why", perhaps recalcitrant, perhaps sly, that so many young people ask of their practicing parents; when the answers are unsatisfactory because legalistic or moralistic, the result is a disaffection that is logical for the young and painful for their elders. But neither group can say what role the liturgy is meant to play in their lives.

There is, finally, another kind of astonishment: that of the young themselves when a meeting happens to bring participation in a vital celebration that is open to the mystery. If the liturgy were always like this (they say on such occasions), we would be ready to go back to church once more. We sense, however, that for this really to happen, their faith would have to be deepened, and they would have to rediscover with clarity and conviction the true nature of life and liturgy, and this clarity and conviction perhaps do not shine out brightly enough in their elders.

When thus cut off from the source, a liturgical celebration becomes self-contained, as it were, without any vital link to before and after. Finding it foreign to them, some turn their backs on it and return to life, their own life. Others persist in crossing the threshold into this foreign world in order that their life may be absorbed into it for a moment or to give their experience dramatic expression. To the former the liturgy is unimportant because their desire is to remain in real life, but what is the life they regard as real? To the latter, life is meant to find its meaning in the liturgy, but in what kind of liturgy do they seek this meaning? The distance remains; the gap is not bridged.

In fact, the unity of liturgy and life is offered to us—"if we only knew what God is offering!"—but it must be discovered and experienced. If it is ignored or rejected, this is because it has not been grasped in its source; for this there may be many reasons, not all of which have to do with the quality of the celebration.

One of these reasons may well be a confusion, hardly realized, between liturgy and liturgical celebration. This confusion is shared by those who continue to practice and those who have ceased to practice. It is even shared by fervent leaders of the liturgical renewal, who focus their entire effort on the celebration and its forms and expressions, the life of the assembly, the texts and movements, the singing and active participation of all. It is necessary, of course, that attention be given to all these; but sometimes they forget what is being celebrated, as if it could be taken for granted. Is it surprising, then, that after so much effort the liturgy still seems to have taken no hold on the lives of Christians? The channels have been repaired, indeed, but what about the fountain?

It seems that the vision with which all these groups start focuses exclusively on liturgical phenomena. But why not begin with the hidden reality, the liturgical mystery? It is possible that a certain type of sacramental theology, the legitimate heir of long centuries of reflection, plays a distorting role in this area. For a long time now, and especially since the sixteenth century, the West has given a privileged place to the idea of efficacy or causality in the sacraments. That the sacraments are indeed efficacious is an established truth, and there is no question of rejecting it. In our own time, however, people are becoming more responsive to the idea of sign; the modern liturgical movement, in fact, owes the best of its pastoral and spiritual advances to it. But were we to limit ourselves to this category, we would imprison ourselves in the celebration without any hope of escape.

Let us return to Origen. Before speaking of ourselves and our celebration, let us begin by listening to him who celebrates and is celebrated. Lest we begin digging our own wells once more, let us welcome him who offers us the living fountain. "For he is here, this Word of God, and his present work is to remove the earth from the souls of each of you in order that your fountain may flow. This fountain is in you and does not come from outside, like the kingdom of God, which is also within you." [4] Before being a celebration, the liturgy is an event. The real question is not "celebration and life" but "liturgy and life". The all-embracing event of Christ is far greater in its breadth and depth and constitutes "the mystery".

---

[4] Ibid., 13, 4.

PART ONE

THE MYSTERY OF THE LITURGY

Chapter 1

"The Mystery Kept Hidden through All the Ages"
(Eph 3:9)

"Then the angel showed me the river of life, rising from the throne of God and of the Lamb and flowing crystal-clear. Down the middle of the city street, on either bank of the river were trees of life, which bear twelve crops of fruit in a year, one in each month, and the leaves of which are the cure for the nations" (Rev 22;1–2).

In this final vision the seer of Patmos glimpses the indescribable energy of the Blessed Trinity at the heart of the messianic Jerusalem, that is, this Church of the last times, in which we are now living. If we let the river of life permeate us, we become trees of life, for the mystery that the river symbolizes takes hold of us. This is the mystery above all others, the one in which Saint Paul sees and contemplates the entire saving plan, which the living God is carrying out in history. We too, who stand at the threshold of its complete fulfillment, are allowed to apprehend by faith its beginning and unfolding. For this plan is revealed, carried out, and communicated according to a wisely ordered economy whose times and dates are determined by the Father.[1]

---

[1] See Eph 3:9. The "economy" is the dispensation, or arrangement by stages, according to which the mystery of Christ is brought to fulfillment.

Of the bosom of the Father, those hidden depths from which the river of life was to flow out at the beginning of time, we could say nothing unless the only Son had himself revealed it to us (Jn 1:18). The mystery "for endless ages was kept secret" (Rom 16:25), and "no one knows . . . who the Father is except the Son and those to whom the Son chooses to reveal him" (Lk 10:22). According to the felicitous formula of the Fathers and the early councils, only via the economy do we enter the theology; that is, the Blessed Trinity reveals itself to us only in its love-inspired plan that is carried out for the sake of man and in conjunction with him. At the end of this book it will also be clear that (as it is put in another patristic expression) [2] only in the liturgy do we *experience* the theology and "know you, the only true God, and Jesus Christ whom you have sent" (Jn 17:3).

He who "has been begotten before all the ages" leads us into the mystery and makes known to us that the living and true God is a Father. For this God, who is the creative source of all that exists, is eternally a source within the Trinity itself. The Father is there the source of the Word, which he speaks, and the Breath, which he breathes. But he is thereby also the source of a communion, for his Son is wholly "toward" him, offering in his reflected glory all that he is and all that the Father has "begotten" in him; the Father's Spirit is wholly "from" him and by his acceptance gives back the gift that he is and that "proceeds" from the Father. In the communion of the Blessed Trinity no person is named for himself. There is here neither "in itself" nor "for itself": terms that among us are signs of barrenness and death. In the communion of the living God, the mystery of each person is to be for the other: "O! Thou!"

[2] Especially in Saint Maximus the Confessor.

Before all the ages the Father is "all powerful", because he is the source of the gift and its acceptance. That is why the one, adorable Trinity is a communion of Father, Son, and Spirit. Here we find life in its eternal outpouring; the river of life, which John contemplates at the heart of history, is an energy of love at work before the world was.

Yes, the mysterious river of divine communion is an outpouring of love among the Three, and in it eternal life consists. Each person is gift and acceptance of gift, never varying yet not motionless; each is an élan that is enamored of the Other but in pure transparency; each is joy given gratuitously and accepted freely. To this communion, with its ebb and flow, to this rhythm of love from which love overflows, no living being can draw near unless the veil of mortality is rent asunder. The human heart cannot contain this inexpressible joy as long as the last attachment to "self" has not been severed.

This river is love, but a love that does not arise in the human heart. This river is life, but a life that does not flow from the human heart. That is because this river, this energy, is wholly other: it is the self-opening of our thrice holy God. Our God is holy because he is wholly other. "Holy, holy, you are all-holy, you and your only Son and your Holy Spirit." [3] The communion within the Trinity is a river of life, that is, of love, because it is holy. When Jesus reveals to us the truth that "anyone who wants to save his life will lose it; but anyone who loses his life for my sake will save it" (Lk 9:24), these words of the Word are infinitely more than a prudential maxim; they plunge us into the very wellspring of the river of life, love, and holiness. And when this river of

[3] Anaphora of Saint John Chrysostom, immediately after the singing of the Sanctus.

love overflows, the manifestation of the hidden holiness will be called its glory. This is the starting point for the economy of salvation and for our eucharistic anaphoras.[4]

In the Beginning

We can enter into the light shed by John's vision only if we move beyond the separating wall of theistic and rational speculations about creation. In the current of the river of life, the breakthrough of created reality into the light of existence is the first phase in what our faith calls tradition or, more accurately, holy and living "tradition" (giving or handing on). In the beginning the communion of love that is the Blessed Trinity communicates itself; this gift *is* the beginning. The Father "gives away" his Word and his Breath, and all things are called into being. Everything is his gift and a manifestation of his glory. Nothing is rightly called sacred or profane; everything is a pure outpouring of his holiness. Our God does not simply do this or do that, like the First Cause whom the philosophers speak of as God; rather he gives himself in everything that is, and whatever is is because he gives himself. He speaks, and the being is; he loves, and it is good; he gives himself, and it is beautiful.

But in this first creation the Blessed Trinity is hidden from sight. From its very beginning the tradition is the mystery of a love that is pierced. The Father gives himself, but who receives him? His word is given, but who answers? His Spirit is poured out, but not yet shared. Creation is pure gift, but one that still awaits acceptance. We often fail to reflect that

[4] See the significance of the triple "Holy" (Is 6) as a prelude to the great anamnesis in the eucharistic prayer.

in this beginning the living God experiences his first "keno-sis":[5] his love reveals itself there, but in the shadow of a promise to which no attention is paid.

Then man appears.[6] It is because God is holy that he calls the man to be "his image".[7] This unique creature, with its male and female forms, is essentially proposed and not thrust into being; it is the only creature that is not "made" but must always be born; it is the locus of the living God's most far-reaching kenosis because it is the treasure he most loves. In the liturgical poem that describes the creation of man God does not say, "Let there be men!" as he does for all other creatures. He says, rather, "Let us make man in our own image, in the likeness of ourselves" (Gen 1:26). This decision contains within it all the risk and expectation of self-giving love: men are called into existence, but will they accept and respond? Will they gaze back into the adorable Face of God?

In the river of life there is a current of tenderness, an incomparable element of attraction. The energy of the holy God, his communion of love, is permeated by an impatient desire, a passion: "to be with the children of men" (Prov 8:31). At the origin of the human person—of each and every human being—there is this outpouring of love within the Trinity, a pierced love that calls us to a life: from the gaze of the Father in his beloved Son there springs up God's thirst, his thirst for men. Thus too, in the very beginning man's nostalgia for God is born. But many stages must yet be traversed before we reach the side of the well where the Word waits for us:

[5] See Phil 2:7, where the Greek verb is translated as "he emptied himself". See *The New Jerusalem Bible*, p. 1941, n. g on this verse.

[6] This coming looks forward to the "Then Jesus appeared" of Mt 3:13.

[7] See the link established between God's holiness and the creation of man in the Eastern anaphoras.

"Give me something to drink. . . . If you only knew what God is offering!" (Jn 4:7–10).

The Time of the Promises

The entire drama of history is located in the tension between this gift and this acceptance: God's passion for man and the nostalgia of man for God. Would men agree to become "trees of life", or would they, on the contrary, claim the right to gather fruit "for themselves"? In fact, history would increasingly become a time of rejection, barrenness, and death; meanwhile, the self-emptying river of life would be silently giving birth to the time of promises.

The Father, "being rich in faithful love" (Eph 2:4), cannot fail to go on giving his Word; the promise is entrusted to one man and through him to many. This is the second phase in the mystery of our self-giving God, in his "tradition"; the economy of salvation is dawning. Through faith men begin to become responsive and accepting and to enter into covenants. The seed of the Resurrection is sown in the time of death.

From Abraham to Mary the Holy Spirit patiently prepares for the first part of the liturgy of the Word, for his hidden prothesis.[8] Saving events now pierce this night of death, as the Spirit gathers a community that experiences these events and raises up prophets who reveal their meaning: Passover and the exodus, the Covenant and the kingdom, the exile and the return of the poor, the temple and the law. This is the time of God's venture in history and his preparation of man for

---

[8] The "prothesis" or "prosphora" is the preparation of the bread and wine before the celebration of the eucharistic liturgy in the Eastern Churches.

the full truth; it is the time of reciprocal searching and of the fidelity of the Holy One that is maintained despite the infidelities of his sinful people. It is also the time when prophetic words and cultic sacrifices are repeated again and again; nothing can do away with this repetition, which signals the grip of death, until the coming of the event that "once and for all" delivers man from death. The time of the promises is a time that runs its course but is still empty, a time that bears the wound of absence but is sustained by expectation; it is a time on the way toward fullness and the presence that lies over the horizon of our nostalgia. It is the time of the luminous cloud but not yet of day. "That day", after so many preparations and prefigurations, will mark the coming of the mystery.

Chapter 2

The Fullness of Time
or
The Coming of the Mystery

Since the beginning of time the river of the mystery has watered the earth to make it inhabitable and to prepare a "home among men" (Rev 21:3; Ezek 37:27). It carried Abraham to the place of meeting with the promise; it has "uncovered the whole way of knowledge" [1] and makes its way through the ongoing course of time. But it could not be given a name as long as "his own people did not accept him" (Jn 1:11); the inexhaustible gift would be recognized only when it was accepted. The river would acquire a name only when it flowed up out of a new fountain. Then the name would ring out like an echo: there would be as it were an encounter of two thirsts that slake each other by giving themselves a name.

The Word Becomes Flesh: The Kenosis of the Son

We are now in the third phase of the "tradition" of the mystery. The mighty energy of the gift that is offered finally

---

[1] Bar 3:37, where the reference is to wisdom as embodied in the law.

36

encounters the other fountain that has been dug and purified through centuries of expectation, the fountain of acceptance, the Daughter of Zion, namely, Mary.

Ezekiel, the prophet of the restoration, had foreseen that
"in those days" water would flow from beneath the temple
(47:1). But its source is hidden. The time of the promise
brings hither its gift: the patience of the just and their faith
amid the night, the psalms of praise and lamentation, the
suffering and fidelity of the poor, a people of hope that is fed
by the word, a sinful people constantly made new by pure
mercy. The entire energy of the gift, patiently poured out at
the heart of Jerusalem, ends here in a fountain whose entire
vital energy takes the form of acceptance. Mary has carried
the Word long before conceiving him and has learned the
self-giving of him whose whole being is consent to the Father.
She has been fashioned by the Spirit and sees without real-
izing it that the most fruitful activity of the human person is
to be "able to receive" God. Now the humble maidservant
can respond to the message with all her being and in the
very words that her Lord used at the beginning of time: "Let
it be!" (Lk 1:38 and Gen 1:3).

Mary says "Yes", and the Spirit who unites the Word and
the Yes, divine energy and human energy, gift and acceptance, comes upon her. The Spirit of the Father is the one
who crafts this Covenant, fulfilled at last, between the Word
and flesh. In the first creation all that exists is "called from
nothingness to being".[2] In the new creation that is beginning here, he who is eternally begotten of the Father is fashioned out of living earth, namely, the entire being of his
mother. "But how shall this come about?" (Lk 1:34): Mary's
question, which is a prelude to all the "whys" of the New

---

[2] Anaphora of Saint John Chrysostom.

Covenant, is given its answer by the Holy Spirit on this first, hidden Pentecost at Nazareth.

He who is to be born of the Daughter of Zion has been conceived not by any "will of man" or by any set of determining causes[3] but by the power of the Holy Spirit. The latter, who is the outpouring of the Father's love, makes his own the energy of acceptance that is operative in the Virgin Mary and renders it fruitful. The age of the mysterious "synergy"[4] between the river of life and the world of the flesh has begun; in the new creation every conception will henceforth be virginal. In the Incarnation of the Word Mary is not simply an inert locus of the event; rather, her entire being as a person is offered, given, handed over to the Holy Spirit. Again, the Father does not stand far off and send his Spirit to carry out his redemptive plan; he gives himself by giving his only Son in his Spirit, who is Love. After the synergy of this first Pentecost, everything is unmerited and personal, everything a manifestation of the Spirit's power. Those who are not caught up in this mystery of the virginal conception of the Word are incapable of receiving the revelation of "what is now to take place very soon" (Rev 1:1), for henceforth it is always in this manner that the river of life enters into our flesh.

Henceforth, everything fleshly is permeated by the energy of love. When the river of life joins the energy of accep-

---

[3] Jn 1:13; "flesh and blood" here is a Semitic way of expressing the determinisms at work in the present world.

[4] "Synergy" (literally: joint activity, combined energies) is a classical term in patristic theology. It represents a faith-inspired effort to go beyond the rational categories of causality (whether coordinate or subordinate) and to account for the utter newness in the union of God and man in Christ and in the Christian life. For those who live in Christ, every action of the Holy Spirit is in synergy with the action of man.

tance, it acquires a name; at last there is a name in which the
Father utters himself and utters his beloved Son: JESUS. Now
indeed joy erupts! The source is here, still hidden in the kenosis, but it has come to birth.[5] The coming of the eternal
mystery shakes our death-marked time and causes it to gape
open; the power of the gift of the Spirit of love and the
power of its acceptance by "the poor woman of Yahweh"
will fill the void. The emptiness will be filled by him in whom
"in bodily form lives divinity in all its fullness".[6] For we are
now in "the fullness of time" (Gal 4:4): the fulfillment of the
expectation that marked the time of promises, the entrance
of the presence of God into "the land of oblivion" (Ps 88:
12), the breakthrough of day into the darkness of our night,
the coming of the river of life into the desert of our death.
And this fullness is Jesus: no longer simply words of the Word
but the Word of the Father in person; no longer a law exte-
rior to man but the grace that comes to birth in our humanity through her who is "full of grace" (Lk 1:28).

"Then Jesus Appeared": The Manifestation

The economy of salvation is marked by a law whose operation we can still verify in our own lives: the "theophanies",
or manifestations of the mystery, are measured by the kenosis of love; the more our God gives himself, the more he
reveals himself. In his Incarnation, the Word "emptied himself, taking the form of a slave, becoming as men are".[7] How,
then, will the Spirit make him known?

[5] See Lk 2:10–14.
[6] Col 2:9. See *The New Jerusalem Bible*, p. 1947, n. e.
[7] Phil 2:7. On kenosis see chap. I, n. 5.

"Then Jesus appeared: he came from Galilee to the Jordan to be baptized by John" (Mt 3:13). He comes to the human in order to be "immersed" in it,[8] with a baptism that extends even to his death. When Jesus appears, the mystery of love that has taken human form in him permeates the sign in which it expresses itself: the river of life, "kept hidden through all the ages", becomes one with the river Jordan. The lowliest and most derisory among the rivers of the world at that time[9] becomes a sign that carries the mystery within itself. Jesus is baptized in the water—that is the sign; the reality manifested is that henceforth the flesh and time, man and the world, are permeated by the Word of life, who has clad himself in them forever.

The fleshly manifestation of the fullness of grace is a mystery of anointing, namely, the Christ.[10] In Jesus the entire energy of love impregnates human energy with an "anointing" that makes this human energy its own and gives it life. In Jesus the Father gives himself wholly, and the Son accepts him. In him everything human is offered up, and at the same time the Father fills him. Jesus is the supreme embodiment of the synergy that will give life to everything, for in him there is no longer a divine action on the one side and a human on the other, but the single action of the one Christ; let us call it a "christic" action in order to bring home to ourselves the astounding realism of the word "Christian". Union without confusion, distinction without separation: that is how the great christological Council of Chalcedon was to put it four centuries later. In the least action of Christ God lives

---

[8] To be baptized, that is, literally to be "immersed".

[9] The Jordan descends from the southern slopes of Mt. Lebanon into the trough of the Arabah (which is 300 meters below sea level near Jericho) and empties into the Dead Sea.

[10] In Hebrew and in Greek the name "Christ" means "anointed".

humanly and man lives divinely, not in a modal union but in the union that is a single person. Throughout his mortal life everything will show forth this marvelous anointing.

When Christ speaks, his listeners hear the man Jesus, and at the same time the Father utters himself in his incarnate Word. Even when faith has not yet penetrated this mystery of unity between Jesus and the Father, the simplest folk cannot but be amazed: "No one has ever spoken like this man" (Jn 7:46). When Jesus acts, even the least and most human of his reactions, and not only his "astonishing" deeds, express some reflection of the mystery of the Father. If Jesus is humble, it is not a "pretense" or an effort to make us comfortable with his holiness; no, it is authentic, with a truth that is not only human but divine, for our Father is humble beyond anything we can possibly grasp. When Jesus weeps, the mysterious suffering of this most loving Father has truly entered into our flesh. The entire Gospel needs to be reread from this theophanic point of view: for each aspect of the kenosis of the Word, that is, our entire authentic human condition, manifests the Holy One of God, who has immersed himself in it. Through the baptism of the Son into our humanity all flesh—every person and community, all of time and the world, all suffering and joy, all death and life—is permeated with the presence of the Wholly Other. Time is irreversibly anointed with his fullness. Even before our response and participation the river of life has reversed the direction of history.[11]

The Father himself puts the seal of his own testimony on this coming: "This is my Son, the Beloved; my favor rests on

---

[11] Hymnology and iconography often interpret Ps 114(113A):3, "The Jordan turned back", in the sense that is realistic at the level of symbol: when Jesus is baptized, the Jordan (the sign) returns to its source (the river of life, which it signifies). The symbol thus returns to its origin.

him" (Mt 3:17). "This man"? Yes, this man whom we see and whom we believe to be the son of Joseph[12] is in fact the reflection of the Father's glory.[13] Because of him every one of God's scattered children will have the power to become the Father's joy and his longed-for dwelling place.[14] The voice from heaven does not announce a promise; it proclaims a wondering exultation at an event that has been awaited for age upon age: the deformed man who had hidden himself far from the Father's face is now discovered again by the Father in his own beloved Son!

This Son is indeed present among men as one unknown to them (see Jn 1:26), but he is nonetheless in their midst. This mysterious marriage, which only the friend of the bridegroom can recognize,[15] is experienced by Jesus in the depths of his heart. Who could possibly have any inkling of the testings and sufferings he had to undergo in order to seal this covenant in the truth of his human heart? For it was in this heart that the drama of the river of life was henceforth played out, and this at every moment of his mortal days. To be inseparably God and man was unceasingly to accept the new life from his Father and at the same time to be heir, through his virginal mother, to all the earthiness of our humanity. It was to be the place where two pursuits, two

---

[12] Lk 3:23, at the beginning of the genealogy that follows upon the account of the baptism.

[13] This accounts for a variant, regarded as apocryphal, in two manuscripts of the *Vetus Latina*: "And while he was being baptized a great light came out of the water"; see *The Jerusalem Bible*, New Testament, p. 19, n. k (omitted in *The New Jerusalem Bible*).

[14] The dove as theophanic symbol of the Holy Spirit in Mt 3:16 refers back to the end of the story of the Flood: the failure of the dove to return signifies that the land is once again habitable (Gen 8:12). The dove at the baptism also signals the beginning of the new creation (see Gen 1:2).

[15] Jn 3:29. The reference is to John the Precursor and Baptizer.

thirsts, meet, the place where two worlds, of grace and the flesh, intermingle. It was to be the meeting point of two loves and the focus of their covenant; the place where two piercing nostalgias met, but also the source of their satisfaction. "Who has given credence to what we have heard?" [16] The fountain is there, and it is the heart of the Savior: place of the Passion of God and the passion of man, place of the com-passion. There God is born in man and man in God: a place of birth and connatural knowledge, a threshold that death is forbidden to cross, a silence filled with outpouring joy. Finally, it is in this heart, where kenosis has achieved its utmost, that the river will arise, and the glory of the Father will be revealed. Then "all flesh will see it" (Is 40:5): that will be the hour of Jesus, the hour when the mystery becomes event.

---

[16] Is 53:1, cited in Jn 12:38, just before the Passion of Jesus.

Chapter 3

The Hour of Jesus
or
The Mystery as Event

The coming of the river of life in our flesh marked the beginning of the fullness of time. The kenosis of the Son in his Incarnation shows the measure of the Father's manifestation of love: it is without measure. Yes, "this is how God loved the world: he gave his only Son" (Jn 3:16). The Word becomes flesh through the Holy Spirit and the Virgin Mary; the kenosis here is a kenosis of the person. Our integral humanity is anointed and wedded in Christ; the kenosis here is total. But it achieves completion only if it accepts our human condition without reservation, including death. "Having loved those who were his in the world, [he] loved them to the end", to the extremity of which love is capable (Jn 13:1). This is the central "moment" in the fullness of time, the "hour" toward which everything before it was moving: the hour of the Cross and the Resurrection. In this decisive "hour" the mystery becomes event.

The saving events brought about by the living God in the time of the promises were simply foreshadowings and stammerings. Even the saving actions of Christ during his mortal life were only signs pointing ahead to his definitive "work". What, then, does it mean to say that our God saves men?

Does it mean that he gives them a course in theology? That he gives them a moral law or even that he gives them the commandment of love? That he teaches them to change structures, whether personal, social, or cosmic? That he lets them know in the smallest detail the kind of worship agreeable to their Creator? That he reveals to them that God is a Father, and kind and merciful, and does so by letting them experience it, as we do with one another in our good moments? But then what?—All that I have just been saying has been the object of the human search for centuries, in religions, philosophies, sciences, ideologies. Heroic practitioners of justice and of love for their fellows have not been lacking in history, even in recent history. But then what?—Even after all this the basic question that holds men in its grip and has found no real answer remains. I exist (says every man), but I exist for death at every moment and in the final moment. Of what use to me are models of morality and fine promises of life as long as the root of this disastrous tragedy—death—has not been pulled up—not tomorrow, but now? This is the only really important question. Everything else is just a passing episode and a distraction.

If the coming of God as a man did not reach to these depths, he would be simply poking fun at us. We would be left with the failure found in all the religions and ideologies: being unable to do away with death, they simply suggest that we not think of it anymore. "The folly that marks the mystery" (1 Cor 1:17–25), in contrast, is that it enters into death. The coming of the river of life into our history is the only truly important event because it confronts the death that lies in wait for us. "No one can see God and not die", the Word tells us since the theophany on Sinai. Were we to reduce this "death" to some kind of sacred fright at the *mysterium tremendum*, we would not only be confusing theology with the pathology of the unconscious; we would also be back where we started, because we would be saying that the human sense of God is still poisoned by death. No, the fact is that "no one has ever seen God; it is the only Son, who is close to the Father's heart, who has made him known" (Jn 1:18). By becoming a man, the Son became "close to the heart of death" and then entered into it; that is the decisive event, in fact, the only decisive event.

In Jesus alone does God become event for man, because in him alone God comes to be with men: not in a half-hearted way by preaching a marvelous good news, but unreservedly, by drinking the cup of our death; not by doing good things for us in a somewhat distant way, thus making us more irresponsible than ever, but by freely offering us a share, even now, in his incorruptible life, provided that we likewise agree to enter into his love-inspired death that alone destroys our death. Jesus conquers death by his death and thereby bestows his life on us—*that* is the most important event in all of history: his Cross and his Resurrection. These are not two events, but two phases or moments of the same mystery.

The Hidden Event of the Cross

There is an invisible consonance between the day of the Annunciation and the hour of the Cross. It is not the congruence one might be tempted to think of immediately: between the first moment of a human existence and its "final moment"; in fact, the hour of the Cross breaks out of finite time. Nor is it the congruence that might be established between the maternal womb in which the Son was conceived and the womb of the earth in which he was to be buried, although each of these conceals the same fontal mystery. No, the invisible consonance of Annunciation and Cross is to be found in the kenosis of the beloved Son. At the Annunciation it begins, and the seed is delicate; in the Cross it is completed, and the ear is heavy with grain. There the Word receives his human condition from his Mother; here he accepts from all men the burden of their sins and their death. Mary, initially the Mother of Jesus, God's Son, now becomes the Woman (Jn 2:4; 19:26), the new Eve and Mother of the whole Christ. The profound coherence of these two births, these two kenoses, is due to the energy of the Holy Spirit; that energy takes virginal form in the coming of the mystery, and it is even more wonderfully virginal in the mystery as event.

It is almost obvious, one might say, that the conception of Jesus is virginal; the scene is permeated by gratuitousness and freedom: the love of the Father and the consent of the Word, the acceptance of Mary and the power of the Spirit. No human volition and no earthly determinism can explain the Incarnation and the kenosis of love that it reveals. But in what sense is the energy of the gift and its acceptance still virginal in the death of the incarnate Word on the Cross?[1]

As the drama of the Passion unfolds, it seems that everything can be explained at the levels of causes and determinisms. The attitudes of the human heart conspire here with factors supplied by the circumstances of the time: the foreign occupation with its collaborators and rebels; the panic of the authorities when challenged and their collaboration for a practical goal; the ambitions and cowardices, the selfish

---

[1] It is to be noted that even though the Muslim faith unhesitatingly accepts the virginal conception of Jesus, it looks upon the death of Jesus as the principal stumbling block in the Christian faith.

dealings and jealousies, the betrayals and denials; the passivity of a silent majority and the demagoguery of a few agitators; the violence and despair. Is not all this just like any other human drama ever played out? How did Jesus come to die? Why, that is much easier to explain than the death and suffering of millions of innocent people today!

And yet all these causes, operating more or less freely, and all these determinisms provide no explanation at all of the meaning of the event. Jesus is the only man who is not caught off guard by death and who does not undergo death as something unavoidable. Not only does he not try to escape it, but he also does not struggle against it, as we instinctively do, in an effort to delay it. No, he goes to death with sovereign freedom,[2] still fully possessed of all the divine and human "health" that regards death with horror. He wills it with the whole of his will as the Son and with the whole of his love for his brothers.[3] He enters into death and, standing alone in the place of all, faces it in an extraordinary combat. "No one takes my life from me; I lay it down of my own free will" (Jn 10:18).

Once again, let us be sure to understand this correctly.[4] It is wonderful that the living God creates *from nothing*, but it is not astounding; rather, it goes without saying. Infinitely more wonderful and even astounding is that the Word takes flesh through the synergy of the Holy Spirit and the Virgin Mary, although in fact the energy of the Spirit can only be virginal. But that the Word of life should hand himself over to death, voluntarily and without putting up any resistance—that is a scandal! And that death should be destroyed *by his dying*, that

[2] The element of freedom is emphasized especially in the fourth Gospel.
[3] On this entire paragraph see Heb 2:9–18.
[4] See chap. 2, beginning.

is the supreme folly![5] Yes, "we are preaching a crucified Christ: to the Jews an obstacle they cannot get over, to the Gentiles foolishness, but to those who have been called . . . a Christ who is both the power of God and the wisdom of God" (1 Cor 1:23–24).

When Jesus is arrested, he refuses to resist; he does not regard his apostles as a bodyguard. When he is struck, whipped, condemned, and crucified, the ingenuous clarity of his words as well as his forgiveness of his executioners shows forth the same mystery. To men who are possessed by deceit and hatred and who bring to bear on him all their power to inflict death, the beloved Son offers no violence, which again is a power to inflict death. He does not want the death of the sinner! On the contrary, he wants the sinner to live. That is why he does not attack men but only the death whose prisoners they are. His nonviolence is neither weakness nor a matter of conscientious objection; it is the power of love. The intention of his enemies is to "destroy the tree in its strength" and "cut him off from the land of the living" (Jer 11:19), but what they in fact accomplish is to raise aloft the Tree of Life whose leaves will have power to heal them (Rev 22:1). At the moment when the kenosis is complete, the nonviolence of love is omnipotent. It is at the very moment when men believe they are "handing over" the author of life to death that this author of life "hands himself over" in order to bestow life on those who are enslaved to death. In the hour of Jesus the divine "tradition" attains to its fullness of grace and truth.

---

[5] It is folly for any anthropology or religion that dodges the issue of death. See n. 1 of this chapter. Anyone who does not live in Christ can only dodge it or commit suicide; see A. Camus in his play *Caligula* and in his *The Myth of Sisyphus*.

In the kenosis of the Incarnation grace dawned; in the kenosis of the Cross it shines forth where the darkness is thickest. These images are perhaps symbols, but they are not hyperboles, because the reality is even more overwhelming. After all, when day dawns, what happens? Night is scattered. Night was simply an absence; it had no existence in itself; nothing produces night, and consequently when it is there nothing exists for anyone; people do not even recognize each other. Night as such is empty of meaning and strips everything else of meaning. Well, at the core of every human event, at the bottom of every human heart, there is a night of death and rupture,[6] of nonmeaning and absence. "Flesh and blood", or mere human nature (Jn 1:13; 1 Cor 15:50), cannot dissipate this night; nothing outside man can introduce light into that blackness. It reigns in the heart and from that vantage point spreads its veil over everything, from the depths of the person to its most conscious structures. Only he who is Light can assume the human without damaging any part of it. And only this Man-God, in whom death finds no complicity with itself, can enter into the thickest darkness of death; that is what happens in the kenosis of the Cross.

In the middle of the day, therefore, "the sun's light failed, so that darkness came over the whole land until the ninth hour" (Lk 23:44). Did the executioners realize what they were doing when they raised the Lord of glory on his Cross? What happened when the Light was immersed in this darkness? Not a romantic dawn, but a struggle, the combat that decided the salvation of all men. Death feeds on lies and engenders lies; it feeds upon appearances and leaves emptiness behind it. Here, at the ninth hour, the hour when dark-

---

[6] The Hebrew and Semitic word most often used for sin draws on the image of the target missed (khata'a).

ness reigns (Lk 22:53), death seizes its prey—only to be throttled by him whom it expects to swallow up. It is "gripped by terror",[7] for he who enters into it is not mortal because caught in the nets of sin, but mortal out of love, mortal by grace and truth. Death has been deceived; its lies have been turned back upon it. When truth shines forth,[8] all lying is shown up for what it is and is scattered like the night before the dawning day. Death is no longer: the Son of the Living God has crushed it by his own death.[9]

The Event Made Manifest: The Resurrection

The fact that the mystery has occurred, has become event, is gradually made manifest. At his coming, at the moment of his baptism, Jesus had seen the heavens open; the Father had revealed that this man was his beloved Son, and the Spirit had confirmed the testimony. Now, in the hour when the economy of salvation reaches its climax, it is Jesus himself who opens "paradise" (Lk 23:43), the garden of life, to men who are straying far from God. He can do so because the source, the wellspring, is now here.

The outpouring of the Blessed Trinity's love shines forth in our flesh: the Father has given himself wholly by giving his only Son and his Spirit without reserve; at the same moment Jesus gives himself wholly to his Father and gives up his Breath for us: "Father, into your hands I commit my spirit. . . . And

[7] See the Easter homily, attributed to Saint John Chrysostom, that is read at the end of the Easter office in the Byzantine liturgy.

[8] See the answer Jesus gives to Pilate: "I came into the world for this, to bear witness to the truth" (Jn 18:37).

[9] "Christ is risen from the dead; by dying he has crushed death, he gives life to the dead" (Easter troparion in the Byzantine liturgy).

bowing his head he gave up his spirit" (Lk 23:46; Jn 19:30). When the Word dies with a loud cry, the veil of the sanctuary is rent from top to bottom (Mk 15:37–38). No longer will men worship here or in some other place, because the true Holy of Holies has now been unveiled: it is the Father's torn heart. The wellspring from which life, the energy of love, pours out is now present: no longer in the form of testimony and promise, as it was when Jesus was baptized, but in silence and full reality, in the body of the beloved Son.

The Cross is the first theophany of the wellspring, and it is because John has seen it with his bodily eyes that he will be able later on to enter into the mystery of it in the final vision of the Apocalypse (Rev 22:1–2). When "one of the soldiers pierced his side with a lance . . . immediately there came out blood and water" (Jn 19:34). "The water flowed from under the right side of the temple" (Ezek 47:1),[10] of the true temple which is the body of Jesus (Jn 2:21). From "that day" forward, "a fountain will be opened for the House of David and for the inhabitants of Jerusalem" (Zech 13:1).

"At the place where he had been crucified there was a garden, and in this garden a new tomb in which no one had yet been buried" (Jn 19:41). There Jesus was entombed. At the first creation, "a river flowed from Eden to water the garden" (Gen 2:10). During the great sabbath of Passover and until the day of new creation dawns the wellspring remains buried in the garden. As the womb of the Virgin received her Lord and her Son at the Annunciation, so the earth receives him now. In the silent depths the final "preparation" (Jn 19:42) takes place. The sabbath is thus brought to its fulfillment in the travail of its Lord; its final act is to pre-

---

[10] When the heart of Christ was pierced by the soldier's lance, the blow caught him in the right side.

vent the embalming of the body of Jesus; all of mortal time was only a "preparation" and is now brought to its fulfillment by the event that is Easter.

For, though all earthly work stops, the Father "still goes on working" (Jn 5:17) to produce the masterpiece of his tradition, or self-giving, of love: he fills with his breath the body of his only Son, who has carried the sins of all and made their death his own, and makes this body rise up alive and incorruptible. This event cannot be described. Any iconography that attempts to describe it can only be a wretched piece of apocrypha. If we could even imagine the rising of the Living One from among the dead into whose absent midst he had descended, we would be making his body still the object of our senses and therefore of death. The silence of the Resurrection is here more than ever the mystery of the kingdom that is at hand.[11] From this point forward, and in his integral humanity, Jesus IS; any element of phenomenality would be a sign of continuing subjection to death. That is why he does not "appear" to his disciples as though he were someone absent who put in occasional appearances; rather, as the vocabulary of the Gospels makes clear, he "lets himself be seen" by them. He does not change form but IS; it is they who, in the measure of their faith, "recognize" him. For the body that rises living from the tomb is no longer simply the body that experiences human thirst; it is now and forever the body of the wellspring of life.

The Resurrection, Manifestation of the Event

"When the sabbath was over" (Mk 16:1)—and this symbol of our cyclical mortal time is definitively done with—the

---

[11] Saint Isaac of Nineveh.

spice bearers could come to the tomb "at the first sign of dawn" (Lk 24:1). Day has already risen: the day of a creation now delivered from death, the day that knows no evening. "Why look among the dead for someone who is alive?" (Lk 24:5). Christ is risen; he is truly risen! Now everything begins.

Life springs from the tomb, more transparent than when it came from the pierced side, more life-giving than when it emerged from the womb of the Virgin Mary. In the tomb, where man's thirst is constantly extinguished, the thirst of God takes it over. No longer is there simply a thirst that seeks the fountain; the fountain itself has become a thirst and leaps up within human thirst. "Give me something to drink.... I am thirsty" (Jn 4:7 and 19:28). The river of life was in a state of kenosis in the mortal body of Jesus; by entering into our death it is able to well up from our own earth in the incorruptible body of Christ. The tomb remains the sign of the extremity of the love with which the Word wed himself to our flesh, but it is no longer the place of his body: "he is not here" is the insistent message of all three Synoptic Gospels. He has become the beginning of the wholly New Covenant struck by the Resurrection. Now the ebb and flow of Passover merge into one; in the risen Christ the incarnate Word is a living man, and the living man becomes child of God. In him the suffering of the Father for mankind is brought to its fulfillment: "You are my son, today have I fathered you" (Ps 2:7).[12]

On this day of birth the river of life becomes LITURGY as it spreads out from the tomb and reaches us in the incorruptible body of Christ. Its wellspring is no longer the Father

[12] This verse of Ps 2 is interpreted in a primarily paschal sense—as referring to the day of the Resurrection or to the Ascension, which serves as confirmation of the Resurrection—especially in the apostolic kerygma and in the catechetical instructions of the Fathers.

alone but also the body of his Son, since this is henceforth wholly permeated by his glory. If it be true that the drama of history is the interplay of God's gift and man's acceptance of it, then the drama reaches its climax, and its eternal beginning, on this day, because these two energies are now joined together forever. The consent of the Son to his eternal birth from the Father completely permeates the body of his humanity. As a result of this anointing with superabundant life Jesus rises and becomes "Christ" to the fullest possible extent. It is this covenant between his two energies, the divine and the human, that makes the risen Christ the inexhaustible wellspring of the liturgy. In the past, the river of life had been in a state of kenosis in his body, being hidden and limited there by his mortal flesh; like the first Adam, Jesus was a "living soul". But when he rises from the tomb he has become "a life-giving spirit" (1 Cor 15:45). Henceforth, in his integral humanity—nature, will, energy—Jesus is alive. He is united to the Father and radiates the glory of God from his own body; being united to the wellspring he gives life (see Jn 5:20–21 and 26–27). The river of life can now flow forth from the throne of God *and* from the throne of the Lamb. The liturgy has been born; the Resurrection of Jesus is its first manifestation.

Let us not imagine this event as being a thing of the past! True enough, it occurred at one point in our history; it was an event and not a symbol. But it also occurred "once and for all".[13] The events in which we are involved happen once, but never once and for all; they pass and, passing, belong to the past. The Resurrection of Jesus is not in the past, for if it were Jesus would not have conquered our death. Above and

---

[13] See Rom 6:10 and the Letter to the Hebrews passim; the phrase is used only with reference to the death and the Resurrection and Ascension of Jesus.

beyond its historical circumstances, which are indeed of the past, the death of Jesus was by its nature the death of death. But the event wherein death was put to death cannot belong to the past, for then death would not have been conquered. To the extent that it passes, time is prisoner of death; once time is delivered from death, it no longer passes. The hour on which the desire of Jesus was focused "has come, and we are in it" forever; the event that is the Cross and Resurrection does not pass away.

More than that, it is the only true event in all of history. All other events are dead and will always be dead; this one alone remains. "Christ has been raised from the dead and will never die again" (Rom 6:9). He was not brought back to life in the manner of Lazarus or the daughter of Jairus or the son of the widow of Nain. These individuals began a mortal life once again and finally died for good. In the case of Christ and him alone rising meant passing through death and passing, with the whole of his humanity, beyond death. He pierced the wall of death and therefore the wall of mortal time. This coming of the Word of life into our flesh and into the very abyss of our death alone deserves to be called an "event", because due to it all the walls of death have collapsed, and life has sprung up in their place. The hour in which the Word with a loud cry handed over his Breath of love so that men might live is no longer in the past; it is, it abides, it lives on through history and sustains it.

This unprecedented power that the river of life exercises in the humanity of the risen Christ—that is the liturgy! In it all the promises of the Father find their fulfillment (Acts 13: 32). Since that moment the communion of the Blessed Trinity has ceaselessly been spreading throughout our world and flooding our time with its fullness. Henceforth *the economy of salvation takes the form of liturgy*.

When seen in this perspective, the question of the relation between celebration and life becomes secondary. The important thing is the relation of both to the paschal event that wells up at the heart of every event. In the living Christ who "is not here" but is risen and who fills all things and holds the keys of death, the heart of God and the heart of man are as it were the two heartbeats of the heart of history. There the wellspring flows.

Chapter 4

The Ascension and the Eternal Liturgy

The river of life, rising from the throne of God and of the Lamb" (Rev 22:1), flowed hidden in the passage of the time of the promises and God's patience. But "when the completion of the time came" (Gal 4:4), that is, when the Incarnation occurred, the river entered into our world and assumed our flesh. In the "hour" of the Cross and the Resurrection it sprang forth from the incorruptible and life-giving body of Christ. From that moment on it has been and is liturgy. A new period thus began within "the present time" [1] in which after its decisive defeat death carries on its war on all fronts but in which, at the same time, the Passage of the Lord continues to penetrate the depths of humanity and history. We are in "the last times". [2]

Just as the hour of Jesus has his Cross and his Resurrection as inseparable phases, so too the "moment" or "date" (*kairos*) [3] that begins the "last times" has the Lord's Ascension and the outpouring of his Spirit as inseparable phases. The relation

---

[1] Paul speaks of the "present time" in contrast to the "age to come".

[2] In setting forth the economy of salvation, the Bible distinguishes the various "times" that make up its implementation: the beginning of time; the course of time (Old Testament); the fullness or completion of time; the last times, in which we are now living; and the consummation of time.

[3] In addition to "times" the Bible distinguishes determining, decisive "moments" or "dates" (*kairoi*) in the development of the economy of salvation; see Acts 1:7 and *The New Jerusalem Bible*, p. 1797, n. i.

between the "hour" and this special date or moment is to be looked for not in their chronological succession (to look for it there would be to remain at the level of dead time)[4] but in the exercise of the divino-human energy whereby the river of life becomes liturgy. Jesus died and rose "once and for all", and that event now lives on through all of history and sustains it. But when in his humanity he takes his place beside the Father and from there pours out the life-giving gift of the Spirit, he does not cease to manifest and carry out the liturgy. There is but a single Passover or Passage, but its mighty energy is displayed in a continual ascension and Pentecost.

The Mystery of the Ascension

It is highly regrettable that the majority of the faithful pay so little heed to the Ascension of the Lord. Their lack of appreciation of it is closely connected with their lack of appreciation of the mystery of the liturgy. A superficial reading of the end of the Synoptic Gospels and the first chapter of Acts can give the impression that Christ simply departed. In the minds of readers not submissive to the Spirit a page has been turned; they now begin to think of Jesus as in the past and to speak of what "he said" and what "he did". They have carefully sealed up the tomb again and filled up the fountain with sand; they continue to "look among the dead for someone who is alive", and they return to their narrow lives in which some things have to do with morality and others with cult, as in the case of the upright men and women of the Old Covenant. But in fact the Ascension is a decisive turning

---

[4] By "dead time" I mean time that is characterized by death and that we perceive as the measure of movement.

point. It does indeed mark the end of something that is not simply to be cast aside: the end of a relationship to Jesus that is still wholly external. Above all, however, it marks the beginning of an entirely new relationship of faith and of a new time: the liturgy of the last times.

We can only wonder at, and try to recapture for ourselves, the insight shown by the early Christians and by Christians down to the beginning of the second millennium, who placed the Christ of the Ascension in the dome of their churches. When the faithful gathered to manifest and become the body of Christ, they saw their Lord both as present and as coming. He is the head and draws his body toward the Father while giving it life through his Spirit. The iconography of the Churches of both East and West during that period was, as it were, an extension of the mystery of the Ascension throughout the entire visible Church. Christ, the "Lord of all" (Pantocrator), is "the cornerstone which the builders had rejected";[5] when he is raised up on the Cross, he is in fact being raised to the Father's side and, in his life-giving humanity, becomes with the Father the wellspring of the river of life.[6] In the vault of the apse there was also to be seen the Woman and her Child (Rev 12); that single vision embraces both the Virgin who gives birth and the Church in the wilderness. In the sanctuary were to be seen the angels of the Ascension or other expressions of the theophanies of the Holy Spirit.[7] Finally, on the walls of the church were the living

---

[5] Ps 117(118):22–23, which is cited in the parable of the murderous vine-growers (Mt 21:42).

[6] In the fourth Gospel "raise up" or "lift up" has a double meaning and applies to both the Cross and the Ascension. See Jn 3:14 and the note on it in *The New Jerusalem Bible.*

[7] One function of the angels in the Bible, especially "the angel of the Lord", is to give intimations of the mystery of the Holy Spirit.

stones: the throng of saints, the "cloud of witnesses", the Church of the "firstborn" (Heb 12:23). The Ascension of the Lord was thus really the new space for the liturgy of the last times, and the iconography of the church built of stone was its transparent symbol.[8]

In his Ascension, then, Christ did not at all disappear; on the contrary, he began to appear and to come. For this reason, the hymns we use in our churches sing of him as "the Sun of justice" that rises in the east. He who is the splendor of the Father and who once descended into the depths of our darkness is now exalted and fills all things with his light. Our last times are located between that first Ascension and the Ascension that will carry him to the zenith of his glorious parousia. The Lord has not gone away to rest from his redemptive toil; his "work" (Jn 5:17) continues, but now at the Father's side, and because he is there he is now much closer to us, "very near to us",[9] in the work that is the liturgy of the last times. "He leads captives", namely, us, to the new world of his Resurrection and bestows his "gifts", his Spirit, on men (see Eph 4:7–10). His Ascension is a progressive movement, "from beginning to beginning".[10]

Jesus is, of course, at his Father's side. If, however, we reduce this "ascent" to a particular moment in our mortal history, we simply forget that beginning with the hour of his Cross and Resurrection Jesus and the human race are henceforth one. He became a son of man in order that we might become sons of God. The Ascension is progressive "until we all . . .

---

[8] The organic way in which Vatican II's Constitution on the Church is developed is consistent with this iconographic tradition.

[9] Byzantine liturgy of the Ascension.

[10] The expression is used by Gregory of Nyssa in his eighth *Homily on the Song of Songs* (PG 44:941c). The entire spiritual life is carried along by this "ascensional" thrust.

form the perfect Man fully mature with the fullness of Christ himself" (Eph 4:13). The movement of the Ascension will be complete only when all the members of his body have been drawn to the Father and brought to life by his Spirit. Is that not the meaning of the answer the angels gave to the disciples: "Why are you Galileans standing here looking into the sky? This Jesus who has been taken up from you into heaven will come back in the same way as you have seen him go to heaven" (Acts 1:11). The Ascension does not show us in advance the setting of the final parousia; it is rather the activation of the paschal energy of Christ, who "fills all things" (Eph 4:10). It is the ever-new "moment" of his coming.

The Heavenly Liturgy

What, then, is this "work" by which the conqueror of death pours out his life in abundance? What is this energy with which the Father and the risen Son henceforth "still go on working" (Jn 5:17)? It is the fontal liturgy in which the life-giving humanity of the incarnate Word joins with the Father to send forth the river of life; it is the heavenly liturgy.[11] In

[11] The expression "heavenly liturgy" is hardly used anymore. Given the concern to demythologize, people prefer to drop it. And yet it expresses a purifying insight of faith that opens us to the mystery of the liturgy. To ignore the heavenly liturgy amounts to rejecting the eschatological tension proper to the Church and either settling down permanently in the present world (secularism) or escaping from it (pietism). This leads in turn to a separation of liturgy from life, for the heavenly liturgy is not a different liturgy that either parallels or serves as exemplar for the liturgy we think of as ours in earthly time. If we ignore the heavenly liturgy, we are at bottom forgetting that the fullness or completion of time is constantly invading our ancient time and turning it into the "last times". Finally, when we ignore the heavenly liturgy, we are situating ourselves prior to the Resurrection and falling back into an "empty" faith. Those who focus on the spatial image in order to reify the

the words of the Letter to the Hebrews, "the principal point
of all that we have said is that we have a high priest [who] . . .
has taken his seat at the right of the throne of divine Majesty
in heaven, and . . . is the minister of the divine sanctuary and
of the true Tent which the Lord, and not any man, set up"
(Heb 8:1–2).[12] This liturgy is eternal (inasmuch as the body
of Christ remains incorruptible) and will not pass away; on
the contrary, it is this liturgy that "causes" the present world
"to pass" into the glory of the Father in an ever more efficacious great Pasch.

This mystery could not be revealed until its consummation was at hand. That is the meaning conveyed by the final
book of the Bible, the Apocalypse, or "revelation" of the
complete mystery of Christ. To us who are living in the last
times, this book makes known the hidden face of history.
There are many hypotheses to explain the book in its final
form, but none denies the noteworthy fact that the vision of
faith expressed in the book develops consistently on two levels. It seems at first glance that, as with icons, we have a
lower level (earth) and a higher level (heaven). But we must
not let ourselves be misled by the literary device. In the
increasingly dramatic movement of the last times, these two
levels are co-inherent. The one that is more obvious unveils
the carnival of death being celebrated by the prince of this
world; the one that is more hidden takes us into the presence
of him who holds the keys of death. The experience in both
cases is an experience of the liturgy.

---

heavenly liturgy or reject it are in fact accepting the old religious schema characteristic of the carnal person—God on one side and man on the other—
whereas the "kingdom of heaven" is already here in our midst and within us.

[12] A reminder of the virginal energy of the Spirit that is at work in the
Incarnation and the Resurrection; the Body of Christ is the sanctuary of the
New Covenant. See also Rev 21:22.

As the very name makes clear,[13] the liturgy essentially involves action and energy; the heavenly liturgy tells us of all the actors in the drama: Christ and the Father, the Holy Spirit, the angels and all living things, the people of God (whether already enjoying incorruptible life or still living through the great tribulation), the prince of this world, and the powers that worship him. The heavenly liturgy is "apocalyptic" in the original sense of this word: it "reveals" everything in the very moment in which it brings it to pass. When the event is present, prophecy becomes "apocalyptic".

The Return to the Father

"I saw a throne standing in heaven, and the One who was sitting on the throne" (Rev 4:2). At the heart of the liturgy, at its very source, there is the Father! He is obviously the fountain both in eternity and since the beginning of time: "the fountain of life, the fountain of immortality, the fountain of all grace and all truth":[14] the fountain that the patriarchs were looking for when they dug wells, the one that the people abandoned for cracked water tanks, the one that drew the Samaritan woman, the one for which the dying Jesus thirsted. But at this point there was no liturgy as yet.

Only when the life that burst from the tomb had become liturgy could the liturgy finally be *celebrated*—only when the river returned to its fountainhead, the Father. The liturgy

---

[13] We should not create an image of the heavenly liturgy for ourselves by freezing, as it were, the characteristics and attitudes suggested by chaps. 4 and 5 of the Apocalypse. The literary device used there is simply a way of opening a door to the mystery; let us not close that door by applying our imaginations on the earthly pattern.

[14] Prayer Book of Saint Serapion (fourth century).

begins in this movement of return. The energy of the gift in which the Father committed himself unreservedly from the beginning; the suffering love with which he handed over his Son and his Spirit; the kenoses that had marked the river of life since creation; the promise; the Incarnation, which included even death on a Cross and burial in a tomb: all this faithful and patient "tradition" of the Father's agape at last bursts forth in its fruit. The liturgy is this vast reflux of love in which everything turns into life. That love had always cast its seed in pure unmerited generosity; now is the everlasting time for giving thanks. "For his love is everlasting!"

"If you only knew what God is offering!" If we only knew how to enter, without any merit on our part, through the "door open in heaven" (Rev 4:1) into the joy of the Father! For the liturgy is the celebration of the Father's joy. He whom we used to fear as Adam did when he hid far from his face (Gen 3:8); of whom we had a mistaken idea, like the two sons in the parable (Lk 15:11–31); or whose ineffable name—"I AM" (Ex 3:14)—we used to murmur amid the cloud—now at last we can recognize him: "He is, he was, and he is to come" (Rev 1:4), and "worship him in spirit and truth: that is the kind of worshiper the Father seeks" (Jn 4:23). The joy we give to the Father by letting him find us inspires the exultation that keeps the liturgy ever alive. How could he, the wellspring, not be filled with wonder when he sees men becoming a wellspring in their turn and responding to his eternal thirst?

Transcending the parables in which Jesus gave a glimpse of this jubilation ("There will be more rejoicing in heaven over one sinner repenting": Lk 15:7) is the reality now attained: the eternal joy of the Father at the return of his beloved Son. The latter had gone forth as the only Son; now he returns in the flesh, bringing the Father's adoptive Sons: "Look, I and the children whom God has given me" (Heb 2:13). The Father's indescribable joy has taken concrete form and embodiment in the countless faces that mirror the face of his beloved Son. In them the joy of the wellspring can break out and leap up and sing like so many echoes and accents made possible by pure grace, and each of them is unique: "In the same way, I tell you, there is rejoicing among the angels of God" (Lk 15:10).

"God's glory is man fully alive." [15] The glorification of the Father began in the hour in which the Son of man was glorified (Jn 12:28). From that point on it continues without intermission.[16] The reason is not only that he has "brought everything together" in Christ "to the praise of the glory of his grace" (Eph 1:3–14), but also that, to his joy, new adopted children are born at each moment as they emerge from the great tribulation. The liturgical language of the Church has from the beginning expressed this glorification in a term that we are rediscovering today: "doxology". The liturgy is essentially doxological[17] in its celebration of the wellspring. The astounding thing is that he from whom the energy of the Gift proceeds eternally should now reveal himself as also an energy of acceptance: from all creatures who are conformed to his Son he accepts the jubilant reflux of the river of life. The celebration of the eternal liturgy consists in this ever new ebb and flow of the trinitarian communion as shared by all of creation: the angels before his face, the living creatures, all the "times" (Rev 4:4–11).

"Ebb and flow": because the Father does not keep this joy for himself when he receives it but causes it to flow forth

[15] Saint Irenaeus of Lyons.
[16] This element of "ceaselessness" in the heavenly liturgy is emphasized in the Apocalypse. See Rev 4:8.
[17] "Doxology" is, literally, "expression of praise".

anew in still greater love and life. The eternal liturgy is thus the celebration of the sharing in which each is wholly for the others. The mystery of holiness has at last turned into liturgy because it is shared and communicated. In its source and in its unfolding the celebration is entirely bathed in this radiant holiness: "Holy, holy holy." It takes the form of adoration.

The Lord of History

Once we have realized that the Ascension of Jesus is the reflux of the river of life to its fountainhead, the return of the Word to the heart of the Father after having accomplished its mission (Is 55:11), we will see how the various biblical images converge, especially those of the Apocalypse, which speaks of the heavenly liturgy in its present operation. The heavenly liturgy celebrates the ongoing event of the return of the Son—and of all others in him—to the Father's house. It is the feast, the banquet, even the marriage, of the beloved and his bride. All is not yet completed, but the great event of history is now present at the heart of the Trinity; there, one with the Father, it becomes a wellspring.

This Covenant at the wellspring is expressed in the central symbol of the Book of Revelation: the Lamb. "Then I saw, [standing] in the middle of the throne with its four living creatures and the circle of the elders, a Lamb that seemed to have been sacrificed" (Rev 5:6). Christ is risen ("standing"), but he carries the signs of his passage through our death ("sacrificed"). His key action in the heavenly liturgy is to take the scroll from the right hand of him who sits on the throne; no one except the Lamb is able to break the seals and open the scroll (Rev 5). Only Jesus, by his victory over death, has accomplished the event that writes history and deciphers its meaning. Apart from his Pasch-Passage every-thing is meaningless. Men can write history, while other men think of themselves as making it. But only he who brings time to its completion can reveal the "meaning of history" by rending the veil of death and deceit. He is the meaning of our history because he is the event that makes it. He is the Lord of history.

All this means that the liturgy of Christ's Ascension is the harvest feast not only of the history before the Ascension but also of ongoing history: the paschal event is constantly bear-ing its eternal fruit in the history that we experience. For the Lord of history is still the "trustworthy" and "true" knight who "in uprightness . . . makes war", whose "cloak [is] soaked in blood", and whose name is "the Word of God" (Rev 19: 11–21). His liturgy is the concrete extension of his victory in the struggle of the last times: "Do not be afraid; it is I, the First and the Last; I am the Living One, I was dead and look—I am alive for ever and ever, and I hold the keys of death and of Hades" (Rev 1:17–18). The heavenly liturgy is the gestation of the new creation because our history is sus-tained by Christ, who is now in the bosom of the Blessed Trinity. It is there that the Lord of history is at every moment the Savior of his body and of the least of his brothers; he calls and feeds them, heals them and makes them grow, forgives and transforms them, delivers and divinizes them, tells them that they are loved by the Father and are being increasingly united to him until they reach their full stature in the kingdom.

The energy that Christ exerts in the heavenly liturgy is summed up by the Letter to the Hebrews in a title that the Letter intends should convey the whole newness of the paschal event: Jesus is our high priest. "'Look, I and the children whom God has given me.' Since all the children share in the same human nature, he too shared equally in it, so that by his death he could set aside him who held the power of death, namely the devil.... It was essential that he should in this way be made completely like his brothers so that he could become a compassionate and trustworthy high priest for their relationship to God" (Heb 2:13–17). "He became for all who obey him the source of eternal salvation" (Heb 5:9). "His power to save those who come to God through him is absolute, since he lives for ever to intercede for them" (Heb 7:25). "As the high priest of all the blessings which were to come . . . he has entered the sanctuary once and for all, taking with him . . . his own blood, having won an eternal redemption" (Heb 9:12). "This he did once and for all by offering himself" (Heb 7:27).

In the iconography of the Ascension the Lord Jesus holds the scroll of history, but he also blesses it with his right hand. Being one with the Father, the Lamb is a source of blessing: he pours out the river of life. Because we are "already" in the eternal liturgy, its current carries us along all the more impatiently to its consummation. For at the heart of the heavenly liturgy is to be heard a groaning cry, that of the witnesses "killed on account of the Word of God"; from underneath the altar they shout in a loud voice: "Holy, true Master, how much longer will you wait before you pass sentence?" (Rev 6:9–10). History did not come to an end with the Ascension; on the contrary, it is en route to its final deliverance; the "last times" have begun. Each time that the Lamb breaks a seal on the scroll of history, the same cry echoes: "Come!" What, then, is this roaring of mighty waters in creation that is undergoing the pangs of childbirth, and in the human body, and even in the depths of the human heart (Rom 8:22–27)? The ebb and flow of the heavenly liturgy ceaselessly draws the world back to its wellspring, and it is then that the river of life gushes forth in its final kenosis: the Holy Spirit.

Chapter 5

Pentecost:
The Coming of the Church

The eternal celebration of the communion of the Blessed Trinity, which has become liturgy in the Pasch-Passage of Jesus, does not take place far off from us. The Ascension of the Lord does not as it were divert the course of the river of life away from our earthly time. Quite the contrary, for from the throne of God and of the Lamb that river pours out upon all flesh in the last days (Acts 2:17; Jl 3:1–5). The Pentecost that came at the end of the new Passover season was itself utterly new. What happened "when Pentecost day came round" and the apostolic group "had all met together" in one place (Acts 2:1)? Let us first reflect on the event; then we shall allow its light to serve as our guide.

The irruptions of the Spirit during the "times" that preceded this day are countless. They occur throughout the entire economy of salvation. They even give the economy its continuity, at once increasingly carnal and increasingly spiritual, until the Spirit effects the coming of the Word in flesh and then establishes him as Lord at the Father's right hand. What happens on this particular Pentecost day, however, is more than one more intervention of the Spirit after so many others: it is a new beginning.

This is not to deny that on this occasion we find the traits that always point to the personal presence of the Holy Spirit and to the virginal power by which he enfleshed the Word and raised Jesus from the dead. Nonetheless, this Pentecost represents a new beginning, for the Spirit is no longer simply the one whom the Father sent with and for his beloved Son; henceforth the Spirit is poured out by the Father *and* his Christ. The river flows henceforth from the throne of God *and* of the Lamb. He will show himself from now on as the Spirit of Jesus and as the power that raised Jesus from the dead. Most important of all, from this day forth he is "given" [1] and will be received and recognized as the gift of the risen Lord. In his very personal kenosis the Spirit will communicate himself as Person. Finally, the Holy Spirit will be "worshiped and glorified with the Father and the Son".[2]

In order that we may receive the event of Pentecost morning, let us recall what happened at the dawn of the fullness of time and then in the hour of Jesus.[3] The continuity will only make the newness stand out more clearly.

When the day of the Annunciation dawns, Mary is ready for her Lord. For years he has been quietly preparing her to live by faith. Her heart, kept pristine by the utterly unmerited favor of God, is surrendered and poor, after the fashion of him whom she is about to receive. When the announcement of the promise reaches her, she is so under the control of the word of God that all her energy of acceptance becomes consent. Then the power of the Father comes upon her; through her and through the Holy Spirit the Word becomes flesh.

---

[1] At his first appearance to the disciples on the evening of the "first day", on the occasion described by some as "the Johannine Pentecost", Jesus gave the Holy Spirit, but the Spirit was not recognized and accepted as such (Jn 20:22).

[2] This phrase appeared in the third- and fourth-century symbols of faith, but it became part of the Creed only at the Council of Constantinople in 381.

[3] See chaps. 2 and 3.

In the hour of the Cross Jesus is a man who is totally assumed by the Word. He too has for years been learning in his own flesh the obedience proper to the Son. He is now wholly a fathomless acceptance of human death, a tree that is uprooted and barren. But he is also wholly given over to the will of the Father; he is pure consent to the Father's love. In this offering that is his death, Jesus is totally a sacrifice that is consumed by love. But this utterly different, holy love transforms without destroying. Only death itself, that illusory absence of love, is destroyed. Then, in his body, "sown" as something "contemptible", and by the power of the Holy Spirit Jesus is raised up in glory (1 Cor 15:42–43; Rom 8: 11). By the power of the Holy Spirit he took our flesh and brought our human condition to its fulfillment; his body is now living and incorruptible.

It is this kenosis and this passage of the Son of God that the Holy Spirit brings to completion on Pentecost morning, but he does so now, and for the first time, in order that "the sons and daughters" of mankind may share in this kenosis and passage. In this sense, too, the beginning is new. When this day dawns, they have "all met together" in one place (Acts 2:1). Who are the "they"? The men who ten days earlier had returned to the city and kept to the upper room, where "with one heart all these joined constantly in prayer, together with some women, including Mary the mother of Jesus, and with his brothers" (Acts 1:13–14). They were simple men who had left everything for Jesus, but they were also cowardly men who had deserted him or even denied him. They too had undergone a preparation for months on end, during which they had seen, heard, and touched the Word of life. They had been called by pure divine favor and then forgiven out of mercy. Very recently they have been listening to his final instructions for forty days, but their hearts, "slow to believe", have made hardly any progress in their three years with him (Acts 1:1–6). The Lord's departure has left them dumbfounded. The bond, weak though it be, that brings them together is their faith, which is obedient and full of expectation. They are perhaps under the control of the word that has been put in their hearts; above all, they are poor. Their "energy of acceptance" grows more intense during these ten days; they dare to hope against hope. They wait, as no man has ever waited before, for that which is possible to God alone. This kind of expansion of human hearts is the final preparation by the Master of the impossible for the moment when in these same hearts the river of life will become a fountainhead.

Then, "suddenly" (Acts 2:2), with the suddenness that characterizes his virginal power, the Spirit of Jesus invades these men and women with his personal presence. They are no longer a group of believers but a new communion. They are no longer sinners but "theologians".[4] They used to be disciples of Jesus; they now become apostles, men "sent" like him by the same Spirit of the Father who anointed the Word in his Incarnation and Jesus in his Resurrection; henceforth an extraordinary power will dwell permanently in these vessels of clay (2 Cor 4:7). "Filled with the Spirit", they continue to be seemingly poor men, but in fact they have been transformed: the life of the Spirit has permeated their nature down to its ontological roots; they share in the divine nature (2 Pet 1:4); they have been truly divinized.

On this Pentecost morning the Holy Spirit has just brought forth virginally the body of Christ that is made up of men, the body that is the Church. The Spirit who proceeds from

---

[4] Byzantine troparion for Pentecost; "theologians" in the biblical sense of Jn 17:3.

the Father has just been poured out by the Lamb who was slain; the eternal liturgy has broken through into our world, and a new creation is now present. The body of Christ is not only present among men but is beginning to "recapitulate" all men in itself.

On this Pentecost day the Spirit turns a little "remnant" of "poor" men and women into the Church. Because the river of life has been received, the liturgy begins in the last times and gives birth to the Church. In this new community the Spirit of the risen Lord is the one who pours forth and draws and sends; he is the river that makes the Church apostolic. But because of him the Church in turn becomes the visible, present, accessible fountainhead that is given to men in order that they may be able to see, hear, and touch the Word of life. It is always in his body that the Word comes to save men. But in the Virgin's womb, on the roads of Galilee, and in the tomb, this adorable body was overshadowed by death. Now that he has been lifted up to the Father, it is from his body again that life gushes forth—but in our world, not elsewhere. The mystery of the life-giving liturgy has not ceased to be incarnate: by reason of the Ascension it entered the bosom of the Father, but because of Pentecost it has entered into the flesh of all mankind. Through the Holy Spirit the liturgy finds "embodiment" in the Church.

"How can this come about?" we may ask. If we follow the unswerving line of the great prophecy of Ezekiel (37: 1–14), which is fulfilled beginning on Pentecost, the answer is clear: the Holy Spirit gives life to men by bringing them into communion. A body is not simply a collection of living members; each member is nonetheless alive only because it is connected with the body. The Church did not come into existence because men decided one fine day to establish a community based on a single profession of faith. On the contrary, the Spirit of Jesus roused faith in the hearts of the disciples and united them to the body of Christ. At that moment the Church was born. The body of Christ from which the liturgy spreads out into the world has existence prior to the members who unite themselves to it. People do not invent the liturgy and therefore do not invent the Church; they come to birth in it and experience it as a reality.

Thus, on this first Pentecost[5] "the dwelling of God among men"—a dwelling which is no other than Christ—became the Church. The Church is not simply *a* vital locus for the manifestation of the Holy Spirit, as were the Tent of Meeting during the exodus and the synagogal assemblies after the exile. The Church is *the* manifestation of the Spirit of Christ in a new community of men and women who have entered into life because the Spirit has brought them into communion with the living body of the Son of God. We know of no other Spirit of the living God except the One who poured out from the side of Christ when Christ gave his life for us and who raised this same Jesus from the depths of death.

The Church is made of the Spirit, water, and blood, if I may so interpret the obscure verses in 1 John 5:6–8; that is, in the Church the Holy Spirit, our humanity, and the humanity of the incarnate Word are inseparably united. It is this "energy" of the New Covenant that is henceforth the

---

[5] There is a tendency today to speak of various "pentecosts" in the Acts of the Apostles and the history of the Church. There have indeed been many outpourings of the Holy Spirit, but there has strictly speaking ("Pentecost" = "fiftieth" [day]) been only one Pentecost that inaugurated the completion of Christ's Pasch, or Passage.

"liturgy"[6] and gives existence to the Church, the body of Christ that is growing during the time of this world. The liturgy is therefore not a component of the mystery of the Church; rather, the Church is the liturgy as this presently exists in our mortal humanity.[7] The Church is as it were the human face of the heavenly liturgy, the radiant and transforming presence of the heavenly liturgy in our present time. Our task now is to gain a better understanding of this meeting of the eternal liturgy and our present time.

[6] According to the generally accepted interpretation of Greek scholars, "liturgy" means, etymologically, "public service". Once the word passed into Christian usage, its meaning broadened. It always retained, however, the notion of a service or function carried out by a group, whence the now popular interpretation of "liturgy" as "action of the people of God". In any case, the element of work (*ergon*) or, better, of energy remains, though transposed to fit the Christian mystery; it is this that interests me here.

[7] This is the ecclesiology that is gaining ground today as a result of ecumenical dialogue.

Chapter 6

The "Last Times":
The Spirit and the Bride

The entrance of the fullness of time into our mortal time places history in a new and paradoxical situation. The hour of Jesus is present, and remains, because in it death is conquered, and life is given. At the same time, however, death is still influential, and the world is still in the grip of its deceit. With the outpouring of the Holy Spirit, the coming of the heavenly liturgy has begun in the Church, and yet we do not see in what ways creation is beginning to be delivered from the servitude of corruption (Rom 8:21). Thus on Pentecost morning the new age begun by the Ascension suddenly enters "this world" with the coming of the Church: this encounter constitutes the "last times" in which we are now living (Acts 2:17) and thus the final stage in the economy of salvation.

The Mystery of the Last Times

The time of the promise bore its fruit in the Resurrection of Jesus (Acts 13:32). Henceforth the fullness of the divinity dwells among men in the body of Christ; through that body our humanity has entered into the eternal communion with the Father. Our own historical time is now "full of grace and truth" (Jn 1:14). This fullness, which is celebrated in the heavenly liturgy, is our "already": yes, in Christ we are already

77

in the Today of God (Heb 3:13; 4:7). The recurring sabbath was the sign of time that is stamped by death; with the Resurrection of Jesus, however, we enter into the day that has no setting. It is this day, this fullness, that the Spirit of Christ introduces into our corruptible time when he comes upon the disciples on the day that brings the feast of Passover to completion. The coming of the Church thus inaugurates the "last times". The two comings—of the Church and the last times—are simultaneous, for the Church is essentially "eschatological", that is, it belongs to the last times; it marks the appearance of the fullness in the emptiness of our earthly time and thus inaugurates the completion of that fullness through expectation of it.

But this coming of the river of life in its hour of fullness is precisely the liturgy. The liturgy, now spread abroad in our world by the gift of the Spirit, has henceforth an ecclesial, that is, eschatological, form. The last times are not "last" in a merely chronological sense, as though they came "after" the time through which Christ lived in his earthly life and "before" his definitive return. The event that is his Pasch or Passage is not behind us but within our time; the parousia is likewise not wholly in the future but has begun with the Ascension and is becoming more complete every day. Our last times are thus watered by the great river of the liturgy that flows out of the fullness of time and draws our times to their completion. On Pentecost the wellspring of eternal life enters the heart of time, the liturgy begins its spread, the Church is born; in short, the last times begin. All this constitutes the newness of the last times, and we are "already" caught up in it.

And yet there is a paradox. "In the final days there will come sarcastic scoffers whose life is ruled by their passions. 'What has happened to the promise of his coming?' they will say. 'Since our fathers died everything has gone on just as it has since the beginning of creation!'" (2 Pet 3:3–4). But one need not be a mocker to admit the brutal fact: sin, death, deceit, and hatred still flaunt themselves as insolently as before. Worse still, faith itself makes it clear that history is traveling ever faster in this direction. Ever since the prince of life deprived death of its rights, the prince of this world has been raging ever more furiously with each passing day. The last times thus still conceal a mystery. It is the role of the liturgy to concretize this mystery and thus make it known to us.

We saw that in the heavenly liturgy itself a groaning cry is to be heard. From underneath the altar those who shed their blood as witnesses to the Lamb shout in a loud voice, "Holy, true Master, how much longer will you wait before you pass sentence?" (Rev 6:9–10). The original injustice has been brought into the light of day: the blood of men, the life they received from their God, is shed unto death; mankind and all of creation are destined for corruption. The blood of all the oppressed people of history[1] rises like a cry, the cry of life itself that calls to the living God, "Cover not my blood, O earth, and let my cry mount without cease!" (Job 16:18). Now, in the fullness of time, Job's outcry has become that of the Son of God on the Cross. It is this that echoes unceasingly at the heart of the heavenly liturgy, and it is this that rends the silence just before the Lamb opens the seventh and final seal of history (Rev 8:1).

The mystery of the liturgy will remain a closed book for us as long as we have not understood that its point of insertion into our history is precisely this death, this cry of shed blood that mounts up to its Redeemer. For we are not living now in the age of Job. The blood of Jesus, which has been

---

[1] And who is not among the oppressed? Oppressors themselves are the first to be enslaved.

shed out of love and not in consequence of some iron law, bears witness henceforth that the suffering of men has been heeded and accepted by the Son of God. More than that, it has become his very own. It has become his as Son of man, but it was already his as Son of the Father. In fact, the mysterious suffering of the Father determined the entire economy of salvation. His first words to Moses already manifested his suffering love: "I have indeed seen the misery of my people. . . . I have heard them crying. . . . Yes, I am well aware of their sufferings" (Ex 3:7). When Jesus' hour comes, he gives fullest expression to the Father's suffering love and in his death reveals himself to be "Yahweh the Savior".[2] Now that the heavenly liturgy has invaded our time, we are clearly not invited to the eternal feast in order that we may distract ourselves from our earthly tragedy. On the contrary, our cry mounts up unceasingly, and it mounts "*from underneath* the altar"; through the blood of Christ this cry gains entrance into the sanctuary (Heb 10:19), and in the same outpouring of love the Spirit is poured out "*within* the last times".

Through the liturgy that waters our world, the Father's compassion permeates the suffering of each man. To mockers who ask what has happened to the promise of his coming, to men who turn away from God because evil is utterly irrational, and to believers who cry to him with Jesus, "Why have you forsaken me?" the Father responds by coming and giving himself without reserve. He comes, as he never came before, each time that his beloved Son is crucified. It is in this Son that he gives himself, and in his life-giving Spirit. The compassion that impels the Blessed Trinity to stoop to every man who dies and give him his life is at the heart of the "last times".

---

[2] "Jesus" means "Yahweh saves".

When I say, as the New Testament does, that these last times are filled by the hour of Jesus, the reader must not think only of the Cross and Resurrection. In this unparalleled event of history there is an often unrecognized "in between", namely, the sabbath. The great Holy Saturday reveals in fact an aspect of the last times and thus shows how profound a reality the last times are. The earth is henceforth left gaping: because the body of Christ is there, death is crushed and can no longer carry on its work of corruption in darkness. Because the Son of God is buried in the earth, the earth is now wedded, and the body it carries will emerge incorruptible. On that virginal day when flesh and blood and man's will to power have shown their powerlessness to give life, the Spirit will give life to all mortal flesh. Our time is henceforth no longer a sealed tomb but is open to the fullness, being drawn into the Covenant and awaiting its consummation. It is the time in which he who ascended to the Father "bringing captives" constantly descends via his Church into our hell in order to snatch from it those subject to death. It is the time of silence before the Lamb opens the final seal of history, the time of hope and groaning, in short, the time of meeting.

This meeting is the one of which the Book of Revelation is speaking when it talks of two levels in the mystery of Christ. As I observed earlier,[3] the two levels are not superimposed one upon the other like the heavens and earth of our mortal space, but are within each other. That which we see becomes transparent and allows the unseen to shine through. "Like someone who could see the invisible" is the description given of Moses, who by faith remained steadfast and left Egypt (Heb 11:27). The description is infinitely more true in our

---

[3] See chap. 4, "The Heavenly Liturgy".

last times. He who is the image of the invisible God has become the firstborn from the dead (Col 1:15–18). He comes to meet man in his tomb, for it is there that the incorruptible body becomes visible to those whom death sought to keep in its grasp. If we remain steadfast through faith in him who holds in his hand the keys of death, we too shall leave Egypt and enter into his life.

The last times, then, are the time of this dramatic and jubilant meeting. In the last times history has entered into the great sabbath of the Christ, the long Holy Saturday during which the Living One communicates his life to the depths. The last times are the mysterious point at which "from their flesh" men can "look on God" (Job 19:26). Yes, we are still wounded by death, but the wound no longer leads to corruption; it is the wound left in the gaping earth, and from it the river of life will flow.

The Spirit and the Bride

Now the final vision of the Apocalypse reveals its full meaning. "Then the angel showed me the river of life, rising from the throne of God and of the Lamb and flowing crystal-clear. Down the middle of the city street, on either bank of the river were the trees of life, which bear twelve crops of fruit in one year, one in each month, and the leaves of which are the cure for the nations" (Rev 22:1–2).

This vision does not take us to a world after the parousia, as is sometimes thought; it has to do with the Jerusalem of the messianic age, before the definitive return of the Lord. We are therefore situated in the last times. Nor is the vision "utopian" (a vision of "nowhere"); rather it is quite localized. This entire passage (21:9–22:2) is concerned with the Church of here and now, because the power of evil still exists, and the nations can still be healed. The last times are here described in their newness but also in their paradoxical character; the fullness is already present in our world, but everything has not yet been brought to completion. The "unfinished" aspect finds expression in verbs of action such as the "coming down" of the holy city or the "rising" and "flowing" of the river of life. The element of "already", in contrast, is expressed in the "finished" aspect of the stative verbs.[4]

However, all the actors in the liturgy, this drama of the Father and men, are involved in the rising and flowing river of life. These are the Father and the Lamb, because they are the wellspring; the trees of life, whose number, twelve, symbolizes the apostolic Church; finally, all men, including the pagans, who "can" be healed by the Church, which healing implies that they accept the gift of life.[5] But the supreme energy, mentioned at the beginning of the cited passage, is that of the rising and flowing river. Here the liturgy has a new discovery in store for us.

It is in fact noteworthy that at the end of this vision (21:9–22:2), in which the Church of the last times is revealed, our gaze is drawn and held by an unparalleled movement: that of the river of life. This movement fills the entire field of vision, to the extent even of making us forget that the vision has to do with the betrothed, the bride of the Lamb. After all, it is precisely in order to show her to him that the angel has carried John in spirit to the top of a high mountain. It is she who is contemplated "coming down out of

---

[4] "Unfinished" and "finished" apply to verbs in the languages used by the Bible. What are conveyed by the verbs are not so much indications of (relative) time as aspects of action or state. The element of "unfinished" also appears in the attitude of the nations in Rev 21:24ff. and 22:2.

[5] And in the case of some that they enter Jerusalem (21:24ff.).

heaven from God" and having "all the glory of God" within her (Rev 21:9–10), and it is she who is then described in lyrical images of light that are unmatched elsewhere in this book. But then, at the end, at the very moment when the mystery is entirely unveiled in sober symbols, we no longer see her. It is the river of life that fills the horizon. What, then, is this energy, this crystal-clear water? It is the only presence that cannot be named and that makes itself known in the utter transparency of the Bride: it is the Spirit.

A saying on love from the early centuries tells us, "You have seen your brother? You have seen your God!" In this light-filled silence in which the vision of the Church of the last times culminates, the angel seems to whisper to John the Theologian, "You have seen the Bride of the Lamb? You have seen the Spirit!" Did not the friend of the bridegroom, and John's master, bear witness, "I saw the Spirit come down. . . . 'The man on whom you shall see the Spirit come down and rest is the one who is to baptise with the Holy Spirit' " (Jn 1:32–33). The "vision" of the Spirit that began in Christ is completed in the Church: "It is the bridegroom who has the bride" (Jn 3:29). The one whom the Precursor points out is the Lamb, and in this Lamb he reveals the kenosis of the Son of God (Jn 1:34 variant). The one whom the Theologian contemplates is the Bride of the Lamb, and in her he reveals to us the kenosis of the Spirit.[6]

---

[6] It is to be borne in mind that each "time" in the economy of salvation is marked by the coming of a kenosis of the love of the living God. It can even be said that this kenosis constitutes it as a time. It is likewise by reason of this kenosis that each time includes saving events. These divine events on behalf of and together with men are thus manifestations of the hidden kenosis. This was already the case at the beginning of time, where the kenosis of God's Word and Breath was manifested by creation. In the course of time the kenosis of the Word was revealed by the promise and by the law, while the kenosis of the Spirit accompanied that of the Son with the gift of faith and the inspiration

For in the last times it is the Spirit himself in person who is sent and given. Pentecost produces the Church because the Spirit of Jesus here begins his ultimate kenosis of love. Henceforth the Church is the "event" that manifests him. "You have seen the Bride of the Lamb? You have seen the Spirit!" The fact that the Bride is transparent for the Spirit to shine through is explicable only because she is the living locus of the kenosis of the Holy Spirit. And she herself shares in that kenosis because it is what makes her the Bride of the Lamb. What the Spirit of the Father accomplished for the Virgin Mary in the fullness of time, he accomplishes now, as Spirit of the crucified and risen Christ, for the Church of the last times. Just as Mary in becoming Mother of the Word incarnate began the fullness of time in her own person by the energy of the Holy Spirit, so too—but this time until the consummation of time—the Church becomes bride and mother through the Spirit of Jesus who dwells in her. This, then, is the last times: the Spirit and the Bride. In this transparent indwelling the Church manifests the Holy Spirit because she is his kenosis. Kenosis and manifestation: this is the unfathomable paradox of divine agape. In this period, which is the last times, all the torrents of the divine compassion flow together into the river of life; the suffering love of the Father and the Passion of the Son pour out into the depths of our death through the kenosis of the Spirit that is manifested in the Church.

---

given to the prophets. When the fullness or completion of time came, it was the Son in person who "emptied himself" (Phil 2:7, the passage from which the noun "kenosis" is derived) and made his our condition as slaves, even to the extent of dying; we have already seen how the energy of the Spirit worked to manifest the Son and raise him from the dead.

Chapter 7

The Transfiguration

If we could grasp the fact that the mystery of the last times is not a mere theory but the hidden drama in which the world and every man is involved; if we could understand that the kenosis of the Spirit in the Church splits, as it were, the nucleus of death within which our hearts have grown hard and our sufferings wither and grow sere; if we would only determine to open the abyss within us to the abyss of plenitude that is offered to us: then the liturgy would no longer seem a mirage or a mere stopping place or a memory. It would become our wellspring; it would become a gushing well within us and bring us to birth as children of the Name we so greatly desire.

"Marana tha! Come, Lord!" (1 Cor 16:22). This cry heard in Christian assemblies, a cry that amplifies the cry of the Spirit and the Bride (Rev 22:17), does not hover over our hellish world as an intercession but rises from its depths as an expression of both pain and hope. Our last times are dynamized by an impatient, loving expectation of the Lord Jesus because, together with the liturgy, the time of the sufferings of childbirth has begun. All men, whether or not they realize it, now stand in a relation to the beloved Son, who came in their flesh, but at the same time they are shaken by a nostalgia that draws them toward this same Lord whose glorious coming is awaited. The radical movement of the liturgy is a movement, in the crucified and risen body of Jesus, toward the "whole" body of the glorified Christ.[1]

The reason for this is that the divine compassion can lay hold of our death and communicate its love to us only by taking flesh among us. It is always in his body that the Word "comes" to save men: not only at his first coming in the flesh and at his Second Coming in glory but also in the time of kenosis in which we are now living. The eternal liturgy, which Jesus celebrates at his Ascension and which takes form in his Church, permeates our world of death and gives it life; but the locus of this encounter and the path its light takes are always the body of Christ. How can this adorable body that lives now with the Father "come" into our mortal condition and become a wellspring of life for us?

The Burning Bush

Moses glimpsed the mystery of this "coming" in the theophany that inaugurated the prefigurative event of Passover (Ex 3:1–6). The name of the holy Lord Jesus was first stammered here as it was entrusted to this man who "saw God".[2] It was made known to him not by a course in theology or by an ecstasy that took him outside the flesh but in a very simple sign: a bush on fire. There are thousands of bushes on the hills of this half-desert landscape, and even a bush that is on fire is not uncommon near camps. The surprising thing about the bush Moses sees is that it is not burned up. He says, "I

---

[1] The "whole body" or "whole Christ", that is, head and members—an expression dear to Saint Augustine.

[2] This is how the Byzantine tradition speaks of Moses on his feast, which is celebrated on September 4.

must go across and see this strange sight and why the bush is not being burned up." It is then that the overwhelming revelation takes place. He draws near to see and he hears Someone speaking. Through the sign that he sees, the mystery of the living God is made known to him: the Wholly Other who flames at the heart of the vision is the divine compassion that shares the distress of his people.

There is here neither pantheism nor a simple process of sacralization, for this presence is the presence of a person. The Holy One does not destroy but penetrates with his fire everything that is. Men are his holy land, and the divine glory permeates it all the more profoundly as the divine salvation draws closer. But the flame that burns us without consuming is not to be comprehended at first glance, no matter how penetrating this may be; it reveals itself by giving itself and becomes known by being received. It is not our flesh that stands in the way of our seeing, as the ancient dualisms claim, but our lack of selfless generosity and love or, in other words, our death. Here everything is given gratuitously, both in the fire that reveals itself and in the heart that receives it. Here everything is full of life. The same mysterious flame burns both in the event and in the heart of the person present here; only in the heart that receives it does the fire become light.

When, in the fullness of time, the light enters the world in person, he who spoke to Moses takes a body and dwells among us. The Virgin conceived, formed, and gave birth to this "body of the Word" [3] by the power of the Holy Spirit; John revealed it as the Lamb of God, the true Passover, and the suffering Servant. But men like ourselves also drew near

[3] Prayerbook (euchologion) of Saint Serapion, bishop of Thmuis (in Egypt, fourth century).

to it. The "strange sight" on Sinai became what the Synoptic Gospels call a "miracle" and the fourth Gospel a "sign", for the incarnate Word is the true burning bush. "Power came out of him that cured them all." [4] This energy of the Word amid our noise, of the light amid our darkness, of life amid our death, is henceforth the fire that leaps from the bush.

Those who draw near to him touch his body, but "his flesh is divine"; those who look upon him see a mortal man like themselves, but his face is "the face of life". [5] He is truly a man; he is truly God. The flame of his divinity does not consume his humanity but illumines it from within and shows through it. His "astounding" actions, that is, his miracles, already bear witness in his mortal condition to the energies that will radiate from his incorruptible body when he rises from the dead. By his miracles Jesus shows himself to be the great and unique sacrament of God for man and of man for God. [6]

For example, one day Jesus gets into the boat with his disciples (Mk 4:35–41); they put out into open water, and, as they sail, he falls asleep. He is not pretending; he is truly a man who has grown tired both because of his human effort and because of the mysterious divine weariness of which the prophets speak (Is 7:13). A squall roars down on the lake,

---

[4] Lk 6:19; see Mk 5:30.

[5] Two expressions used by Saint Gregory of Nyssa in his *Life of Moses*.

[6] When the first Christian community subsequently wrote down these miracles, it was "reminded" by the Spirit of their fleshly and historical coherence, but it was also guided by the Spirit to "the complete truth" about their abiding meaning, for it is in this way that the risen Lord continues to live among us in the last times. Understanding of the "spiritual meaning" of Scripture does not come through sophisticated thinking; rather the wholly simple energy of the Spirit reveals it by making Christians experience it. This is precisely one of the fruits of the liturgy.

and the waves crash over the boat and soon fill it. Then, like Moses, the disciples "draw near": "Master, do you not care? We are lost!" How could he himself be anxious? In the midst of the storm he is, even in his humanity, the One in whom all things have their being and who holds all things in his hand. Nonetheless, in a movement that acquires its full meaning in the light of his Resurrection, he "awakes" and "arises". With his bodily lips the Word who at every instant calls all things from nothingness into being says to the sea: "Quiet now! Be calm!" The wind drops, the waves quiet, and there is a great calm.

In this storm we are no longer at the dawn of creation but in the tragic time of human salvation; the divine energy no longer acts alone but, in the body of Christ, acts in synergy with a man; that is why Jesus is the great sacrament. For when the love of our God acts in our behalf, it calls for our cooperation, that is, our faith. But that faith, still very timid indeed, was present in the worried hearts of the disciples. They were afraid, these men of little faith; if Jesus nonetheless asks them, "Have you still no faith?" it is in order to liberate that faith from fear and to make it grow. Then they are overwhelmed by the awe that allows faith to expand and open itself to the divine presence: "Who can this be?"

The external setting at that time was a storm on Lake Tiberias; today it is new and different at every moment, but that changes nothing essential; the important thing is the event that is experienced, now as then, by the Word together with men, and this event always takes place in his body. Whether in the fullness of time or now in the last times, the body of the Lord Jesus is the sacrament that gives life to men. To convince ourselves of this, we must once more ascend a mountain, where the theophany of the burning bush finds its counterpart and fulfillment.

The Transfiguration[7]

The Synoptic writers deliberately make this "strange sight" the high point of the ministry of Jesus.[8] The astonishment felt and the questions roused by the preceding theophanies— "Who can this be?" "Who do you say I am?"—lead to this summit, and it is from here that the journey to the final Passover in Jerusalem begins. The miracles were anticipations of the energies of the risen Christ; the transfiguration is the theophany that reveals their meaning or, better, that already brings to pass what these energies will accomplish in our mortal flesh: our divinization.

The transfiguration is the historical and literary center of the Gospel by reason of its mysterious realism: the humanity of Jesus is the vital place where men become God. Christ is truly a man! But to be a man does not mean "being in a body", as all the unrepentant dualisms imagine; according to biblical revelation, it means "being a body", an organic and coherent whole. Because men are their bodies, they are also, like their God, related to other persons, the cosmos, time, and him who is communion in its fullest possible form. Moreover, ever since the Word took flesh he has a "human" relationship, with all its dimensions, to the Father and to all other men: the fire of his light sets the entire bush aflame; the whole

---

[7] Christians are still too likely to misunderstand this event and look upon it as just one miracle among others, a kind of apologetic proof. The feast celebrating it has likewise become indistinct to them, perhaps because it is the only one not to have a place in the chronological sequence of the Lord's feasts. It is a commemoration of an event that occurred during his mortal life, but it is celebrated after Pentecost and in the bright light of summer (August 6). Yet this event, which upsets the logic that we see as governing time, is precisely the one that best brings home to us the eschatological condition of the body of Christ; it is an apocalyptic vision at the center of the Gospel.

[8] Mk 9:2–10; Mt 17:1–9; Lk 9:28–36.

of his humanity is "anointed" with it; "in him, in bodily form, lives divinity in all its fullness" (Col 2:9), and to this Paul adds, "and in him you too find your own fulfillment" (v. 10).

What was it, then, that took place in this unexpected event? Why did the Incomprehensible One allow his "elusive beauty" to be glimpsed for a moment in the body of the Word? Two certainties can serve us as guides. First, the change, or, to transliterate the Greek word, the "metamorphosis", was not a change in Jesus. The Gospel text and the unanimous interpretation of the Fathers are clear: Christ "was transfigured, not by acquiring what he was not but by manifesting to his disciples what he in fact was; he opened their eyes and gave these blind men sight".[9] The change is on the side of the disciples. The second certainty confirms this point: the purpose of the transfiguration, like everything else in the economy that is revealed in the Bible, is the salvation of man. As in the burning bush, so here the Word "allows" the light of his divinity "to be seen" in his body, in order to communicate not knowledge but life and salvation; he reveals himself by giving himself, and he gives himself in order to transform us into himself.

But if it be permissible to take off the sandals of curiosity and inquisitive gnosis and draw near to the mystery, we may ask: Why did Jesus choose this particular moment, these two witnesses, and these three apostles? What was he, the Son—so passionately in love with the Father and so passionately concerned for us—experiencing in his heart? A few days before Peter had already been given an interior enlightenment and had acknowledged Jesus as the Christ of God. Jesus had then begun to lift the veil from the not far distant ending of his

---

[9] Saint John Damascene, *Second Homily on the Transfiguration* (PG 96:564C).

life: he had to suffer, be put to death, and be raised from the dead. It is between this first prediction and the second that he undertakes to ascend the mountain. The reason for the transfiguration can be glimpsed, therefore, in what the evangelists do not say: having finished the instruction preparatory to his own Pasch, Jesus is determined to advance to its accomplishment. With the whole of his being, the whole of his "body", he is committed to the loving will of the Father; he accepts that will without reservation. From now on, everything, up to and including the final struggle at which the same three disciples will be invited to be present, will be an expression of his unconditional "Yes" to the Father's love.

We must certainly enter into this mystery of committed love if we are to understand that the transfiguration is not an impossible unveiling of the light of the Word to the eyes of the apostles, but rather a moment of intensity in which the entire being of Jesus is utterly united with the compassion of the Father. During these decisive days of his life he becomes transparent to the light of the love of the One who gives himself to men for their salvation. If, then, Jesus is transfigured, the reason is that the Father causes his own joy to flame out in him. The radiance of the light in the suffering body of Jesus is, as it were, the thrill experienced by the Father in response to the total self-giving of his only Son. This explains the voice that pierces through the cloud: "This is my Son, the Beloved; he enjoys my favor. Listen to him" (Mt 17:5).

We can also understand the profound feelings of Moses and Elijah, for these two men who had sensed the closeness of the divine glory that was impatient to save man are now contemplating it in the body of the Son of Man. "I have indeed seen the misery of my people.... I have heard them crying for help.... I am well aware of their sufferings, and I have come down to rescue them" (Ex 3:7–8); "Answer me,

Yahweh, answer me. . . . I am full of jealous zeal for Yahweh Sabaoth, because the Israelites have abandoned your covenant" (1 Kings 18:37; 19:10). All this is expressed now not by divine words or human words but by the Word himself in his humanity. No longer is there only promise and expectation, for the event has occurred; there is now present "the reality·. . . the body of Christ" (Col 2:17). Moses and Elijah can leave the cave on Sinai without hiding their faces, for they have contemplated the source of light in the body of the Word.

The three disciples, for their part, are flooded for a few moments by that which it will be granted to them to receive, understand, and experience from Pentecost on, namely, the divinizing light that emanates from the body of Christ, the multiform energies of the Spirit who gives life. The thing that overwhelms them here is that "this man" is not only "God with men" but God-man; *nothing can pass from God to man or from man to God except through his body*. Peter will bear witness in his Letters, as John does in all his writings, to the second of the two certainties I mentioned earlier: that participation in the life of the Father that pours out from the body of Christ is *measured by the faith of the human recipient*. The new element in the transfiguration consists in this light of faith that has given their bodily eyes the power to see. Thanks to this light, they "touch the Word of life" when they draw near to the body of Jesus.

Henceforth there is no longer any distance between matter and divinity, for in the body of Christ our flesh is in communion (without confusion or separation) with the Prince of life. The transfiguration of the Word gives a glimpse of the fullness of what the Word inaugurated in his Incarnation and manifested after his baptism by his miracles: namely, the truth that the body of the Lord Jesus is the sacrament that gives the life of God to men. When our humanity consents without reserve to be united to the humanity of Jesus, it will share the divine nature (2 Pet 1:4); it will be divinized. Since the whole meaning of the economy of salvation is concentrated here, it is understandable that the liturgy should be the fulfillment of the economy. The divinization of men will come through sharing in the body of Christ.

The Sacramental Liturgy

In light of what has been said, we can understand why the constant tradition of the Eastern Churches regards the transfiguration as the event that is the source of the sacramental liturgy. The body of Jesus is not merely a sign of God's presence, as the bush on Sinai was, or merely an inert receptacle of the divinity, as our unwitting Nestorians imagine. It is a sacrament; it is "anointed" with the divine nature in the unity of the person of the Son. Because the humanity of Jesus is "filial" in every fiber of its being and in his love-inspired consent, it can make its own the least movements and deepest wounds of our humanity and fill them with the life of the Father. The divinizing energies of the body of Christ will reach us henceforth in our entire being, in our "body". When the Lord then takes one or other of our fleshly realities— water, bread, wine, oil, man and woman, the contrite heart—he links it to his growing body and causes it to share in his life-giving influence. What we call the sacraments are in fact the divinizing actions of the body of Christ in our own very humanity. In a fully realistic spiritual sense, these energies are sacramental, for otherwise they could not divinize us. We can receive the Spirit of Jesus only because Jesus assumes our body.

During his earthly life Jesus could not attain to the full development of his power to divinize; he was limited in his relationships, not by his body as such but by its mortality. Once he had conquered death, these limitations were transcended and abolished. In this sense, the body of Christ became fully "sacramental" as a result of the Cross and Resurrection. "By his Ascension", says Saint Ambrose, "Christ passed into his mysteries", that is, acquired his sacramental energies. The "passage" was that of his Pasch. Consequently, although the body of Christ was a sacrament from the moment of the Incarnation, it became such, fully and without limitation, through his Resurrection and Ascension. Thenceforth, and forever, he is the sacrament of the communion between God and man.

Some people imagine that Christ, as sacrament of human salvation, is "up there"; that the Church is another sacrament, "down here"; and, finally, that there are the sacraments of the Church, which are celebrated from time to time. This schema, I suspect, is one of the reasons for the divorce of liturgy from life. No, there is but a single body of Christ that is a great and unique sacrament. The wonderful truth that we must constantly rediscover is that the same Lord who allowed his three disciples to participate in his divinizing light, at a time when his body was still mortal, continues now, with an infinitely greater exercise of power, to divinize men in his very body, which is the Church. If his body did not share our mortal condition, how could we be divinized? But this living body is the Church.

The Church is in actuality the state of kenosis in which the flesh of the Word communicates life to the world until the day when death is destroyed forever (1 Cor 15:26). Since his Ascension the Lord has been pouring out the river of life—the liturgy—on men in his body, which is the Church.

That is the transfiguration continuing today. The paradox of the last times is brought to focus in the ongoing, dynamic event of Christ's transfiguration; in this event the sacramental liturgy has its fulfillment.

The reason is that between Tabor and today the Resurrection, the outburst of glory, has taken place, and the Holy Spirit has come. It is thanks to the kenosis of the Holy Spirit in the Church that faith can spring to life in our very weakness, and our eyes can be opened so that we may recognize the Lord and be transformed into him. We no longer need the cloud in order to hear the Father and draw near to Jesus; the humanity of the Church is the body in which the Lord now reveals himself and acts, for in his Holy Spirit our humanity and his have become a single body.[10]

This, then, is the body of Christ, the sacrament of human salvation and God's glorification. The liturgy creates in the Church the transfiguration of the "whole body", which is now growing, the transforming union in which men become God. It is in this light that we can understand the classic definition of the liturgy as the "energy of the people of God". The "energy" here does not proceed from the Church as a separate entity alongside or after Christ; it is the synergy of the Man-God as communicated to his Church in the Holy Spirit; it is the union without confusion, the confluence of the energy of the Gift and the energy of acceptance, the virginal and all-powerful meeting of two gratuities. The humanity in which this energy takes hold is thus no longer flesh and blood, or a sociological group, or a set of structures; rather it "becomes" the people *of* God; it becomes the

---

[10] Everything we saw in chap. 5 on Pentecost as the coming of the Church finds its confirmation here. The apostles became the body of Christ, and this same body grows constantly through time; the "apostolic" Church is the sacramental Church.

body *of* Christ. This "becoming" is precisely the event of the transfiguration.

What, then, is this extraordinary power that flows from the body of the Lord and in which we can participate, even now and in our human reality? What are these divinizing energies that in the liturgy gradually "transfigure the wretched body of ours into the mold of his glorious body" (Phil 3: 21)? This is what we must still learn if we are to receive the fontal liturgy.

Chapter 8

The Holy Spirit and the Church
in the Liturgy

When we approach the body of the Lord, the first source of
amazement to us should be the fact that we have been drawn
to him. It is the Father who has thus "drawn" us (Jn 6:44),
and, in our impoverished but loving faith, his passionate love
for his beloved Son has to some extent become ours. As
soon as we consent to enter into the cloud of faith, he reveals
Jesus to us as the only reality. "Suddenly, when they looked
round, they saw no one with them anymore but only Jesus"
(Mk 9:8); Jesus by himself is everything.

In this body of Christ "all things hold together.... God
wanted all fullness to be found in him" (Col 1:17,19). In
him the Father's joy is poured out on all men; each man is
loved in a unique way and can become once again a source
of glory for the Father. In him is the life of all creatures. He
is our life and our resurrection; therefore, "Lord, to whom
shall we go?" (Jn 6:68). In him mankind is restored, and
men are reconciled; he has "destroyed in his own person the
hostility" (Eph 2:14ff.). In his transfiguration this adorable
body cannot but henceforth vibrate with joy; the liturgy is
the overflow of his life-giving Spirit.

For the Holy Spirit, whose eternal source is the Father, is
sent from the beginning of time together with the Son and
for the Son. He is the maternal envoy of the Father to men,

sent in order that they may know the Son, be incorporated into him, and share his life. That is why he is present in human hearts as the attraction that the Father exerts to draw them to Jesus; as the Father's passionate love for his Son and for all his children; as the Father's communion poured out lavishly. In the body of Christ and flowing forth from it, the Holy Spirit is, as it were, the impatient desire of the Father's glory that men should live. In this body, which has overcome the limitations of death, the Spirit acts henceforth with power. And when he elicits our response to his multiform energy, the Spirit and the Church become one in an astounding "synergy":[1] the liturgy.

The Light with Its Threefold Extension

In the liturgical icon that depicts the transfiguration of Christ for our faith to gaze upon, the wellspring is pure light and opens up a new, unbounded space in which everything is

---

[1] We have met this word before (chap. 2, n. 3), and it will occur frequently from now on. Readers will understand my preferring it to "cooperation" (an equivalent term derived from Latin), since the connotations of the latter are quite different in the modern languages. The "synergy" of the Holy Spirit and the Church is a key idea for an understanding of the mystery of the liturgy. It has its foundation in Christ himself. Being true God and true man, Jesus has two wills (contrary to the Monothelite heresy) and two operations, or "energies" (contrary to the Monoenergist heresy), which de facto are in unison, but freely so and without confusion. Thus Christian sanctity is wholly located in the divinization of our nature in Christ (see chap. 16) through the union of our wills with that of the Father in Christ and through the "synergy" of the baptized and the Holy Spirit in every vital action. This union of wills is love in operation; see Eph 2:9 and Phil 2:13. Once a certain depth of transforming union is reached, the strong words of Saint John of the Cross become applicable: "God and his work is God" (Maxim 157).

penetrated by the light radiating from the body of the Lord.[2] This space that dispels the shadow of death is the liturgy. From the incorruptible body the pure light of the one, holy, and indivisible Trinity emanates. But the saving radiance of its glory reaches all beings through multiple energies, and these are the energies of the Holy Spirit. The light of the transfiguration is single in its mystery but threefold in its radiation, according to the three times of the economy of salvation that the body of Christ experiences.

Since the body of the Lord Jesus is the sole reality and since the fullness dwells in it, the first energy of the Spirit will have for its action to *manifest* it to us. He, the Lamb of God, is present; he comes into our world, but so many images hide him from us still, and the darkness of deceit turns us away from him. Then the Paraclete, the new precursor of Jesus' coming in glory, will purify our vision with his silent light; he will bring us from our carnal views to the pure knowledge of faith. The Holy Spirit springs from Christ as the *fullness of time* and gives us a participation in him. He transfigures us by first enlightening the eyes of our hearts. We then become, even more than the disciples at Emmaus, *contemporary* with the hour of Jesus. This is the Today of the liturgy.

Having awakened us to the unmerited gift of faith, the Holy Spirit can penetrate with his life-giving light the deformed image of man and transfigure it. He can reach into our darkness where death is entrenched. If the Light gives us a participation in itself by becoming our faith, it does so in order that we may offer our whole being to it and become increasingly light. This energy, we sense, reaches into the

[2] This is a constant, whether the iconography be Armenian, Coptic, Greek, Roman, Slavic, or Syrian.

very depths of our mortal condition; it is the energy proper to the *last times*, the energy by which the Holy Spirit seeks to *transform* us into the glorious body of the Lord.

Finally, if we are given the gift of "believing in his name" and if we have received "power to become sons of God" (Jn 1:12), it is in order that he may send us into this world as he himself was sent by the Father. His Spirit gives us a new birth in order that his glory may be manifested to others through us and that they in turn may be transformed into the body of the Lord. This final extension of the life-giving light is intended to *communicate* the reality that is the body of Christ and introduce into communion with it the scattered children of God. In this third energy the Spirit and the Church are bound together in the closest possible synergy because they entrust themselves to one another in a single mission of love. This is an authentic anticipation of the *consummation of time*, in the sense that the Spirit and the Church give the experience even now of the mystery of the kingdom and hasten its coming.

The Manifestation of the Body of Christ

The primary tragedy of history is that the Word comes among men as their light and their life, and they do not recognize him. He is in our midst, in the reality of his body, as one whom we do not know (Jn 1:9f., 26). The reason is that he cannot be known from outside, since exteriority is the wound afflicting our mortal knowledge. The miracle the Spirit works is to reveal him to us from within, not by means of a technique reserved to initiates but through the personal commitment of anyone who receives him. That is why the first person to whom the Holy Spirit manifests the body of the Word is his Mother, the Virgin Mary: she recognizes her Son and her God because she conceives him in faith and carries him in hope. In the fullness of time, then, she is the Church in her own person.

Now that the Church has become a reality at Pentecost, the same pattern holds: the Spirit manifests Jesus to those who are poor enough to believe in him, leave everything for his sake, and become capable of carrying him within them in tribulation. The energy of the Holy Spirit does not operate by giving us ideas about Christ but by purifying our hearts for him. The body of the Lord becomes the primary and blindingly evident fact of our lives to the extent that we renounce ourselves and seek him in love. This is the first synergy by which the Spirit transforms us into disciples and theologians, not through "discourse about God" but through loving faith in his Christ.

The fourth Gospel opens with a week in which John the Theologian describes the first encounters with Jesus and does so with the freshness and exact detail of love. In these chapters we can follow the series of illuminations that the Holy Spirit causes in the hearts of these poor men who have no pretensions to learning. The starting point is the gaze that John the Baptist directs at Jesus. We sense that it is bathed in the light with which the Spirit transfigured it at the baptism of Jesus. That is why John recognizes the Lamb of God as he sees him coming toward him and why on the next day he again directs his gaze at him. It is at this point that two of John's disciples begin to follow Jesus. Who will ever grasp the depth of this gaze of the bridegroom's friend, a gaze so purified by expectation and so communicative of divine love that his two disciples leave him, "drawn" by this man before whom their master retires into the background? The Virgin and the Church undoubtedly do plumb the depths of that gaze, for the Spirit is the light that enlightens the Bride and reveals her Lord to her (Rev 21:23).

"Come and see." The first two disciples were looking for the place where their new rabbi was staying; they "find the Messiah" and then spread to others the light that has drawn them. Now it is the gaze of Jesus himself that begins to beam the light of the Holy Spirit into the hearts of Peter, Philip, and Nathanael; it is he who "knows" them and turns their lives upside down. Jesus enables them to glimpse the evidence that will allow faith to be born in them: he shows himself to them not as the "Son of God" or as the King of Israel whom they had imagined for themselves, but as the humiliated and glorified Son of Man, who in his Ascension pours out life upon the world. This week of theophanies ends with the first "sign" by which Jesus manifests his glory and anticipates his hour, the outpouring of his Spirit, and the marriage of the Church.

Until the transfiguration the Holy Spirit will go on purifying the gaze of the disciples in the light of their first expectation: "Whom do you seek?" "Who is this man?" "But you, who do you say I am?" "What about you, do you want to go away too?" Despite Peter's confession and the predictions of the Passion and Resurrection, they understand nothing: the Spirit is at work in their hearts, but he is not yet given or recognized as long as the body of Jesus has not extended itself by accepting and destroying our death. On the morning of the Resurrection, only one person sees and believes despite appearances: the disciple whom Jesus loved. A little later, it is this same disciple who through the morning mist is able to recognize the distant, shapeless figure of the Lord, because his love for his Lord has forever transformed his vision. The entire witness of this disciple flashes forth in concentrated form in the final Beatitude of the Gospel:

"Blessed are those who have not seen and yet believe." The Spirit awakens awareness of this Beatitude in the heart of the Church, who henceforth sees with her eyes, contemplates, touches with her hands, and proclaims the Word of life (1 Jn 1:1–3). It is to her again that the Spirit reveals her coming Lord: "Do not be afraid; it is I, the First and the Last; I am the Living One. I was dead and look—I am alive for ever and ever" (Rev 1:17–18).

If the risen Lord is in our world as the reality outside of which everything is empty and absurd, how is it that we rub shoulders with him "without recognizing his body" (1 Cor 11:28–29)? We need only acknowledge that we are blind from birth, and his Spirit will enlighten us; but if we claim to see, our sin remains (Jn 9:39ff.). The Holy Spirit teaches us the humility of heart that reaches beyond the limits of all our "external knowledge". It is not through a kind of newspaper account or through an empirical reading or unconscious experience of events that we shall discover Christ, even though it is precisely in these events that he comes and that his Spirit is at work. Nor can the Spirit act through our subjective interpretations of events, for the meaning we give to them is aimed only at preserving our balance; it throttles the nostalgia that would alert us to the coming of the Lord.

When events shake us like fissures suddenly opening before us into the abyss of death, what do we do? Either we retreat to the two positions already mentioned, or we venture on to two other paths, distracting ourselves in order to survive. Some choose science and technology, but to know the chain of causation and even to control it is not yet to have discovered its meaning. Others, wishing to find out why absurd death seizes everything human in its claws, choose the search for meaning and take their disquiet seriously, until they reach the uncrossable threshold of the question that is concealed in every event: Are we to be the slaves or the conquerors of death? But these are not ideas that can exorcise death in its countless forms.

The light energy of the Holy Spirit does not exclude these planes of vision; it penetrates them, discerns them, and finally makes them burst open, as it were, in the event that is already there: the adorable body of Christ in which death has been overcome and which offers us life. Authentic Christian prophetism resides in this discernment, which leads to shattering conversion: The Lord is here and is coming, given to us as promise of Resurrection at the heart of every event. With this as his point of departure, the Spirit carries on an inexhaustible pedagogy, for the discovery of the Lord is always new. "In the measure of our faith" this synergy of Light will lead us from conversion to conversion. Love alone gives sight and the power of discovery. The Spirit will make the body of Christ known to us until it fills our entire field of vision: nothing is alien to it, as we shall see in the lived liturgy. But—to get back to the source of light in us—the Spirit teaches us first to rediscover the way of the heart, where he pours himself out in us and where prayer becomes life itself.

The Passage of the Body of Christ

All of "the wonderful works of God" contain a meaning that the Spirit reveals because he is their author. The meaning is embodied in Christ, but it is his Breath that breathes it into him. Christ is the reality, but the Spirit is its maker. It is he whom the Lord Jesus pours out on "those who believe in his name" in order that they may have "power to become children of God" (Jn 1:12). The second energy of the Spirit operates to transform us into Christ, "into the image that we reflect in brighter and brighter glory; this is working of the Lord who is the Spirit" (2 Cor 3:18).

On Tabor the disciples experienced the divinizing enlightenment "in the measure of their faith". The same holds for us today in the transfiguration that is the liturgy. The Holy Spirit transforms everything he touches, but his energy will be all the more transformative as our faith is more naked and sacrificial. Here is where the decisive event of the liturgy takes place. In an effort to say the ineffable, the tradition of the apostolic Churches tells us of this event in a word that seeks to capture the utterly gratuitous thrust of faith: epiclesis. An "epiclesis" is an appeal to the Father to send his Holy Spirit on what we are offering to him so that this Spirit may change the offering into the reality of the body of Christ. The word "epiclesis" expresses the emptiness that is set before God; it cannot express the fullness that is given to us. It expresses the groan of appeal, not the silent love that answers it. For appearances remain unchanged as long as we are in this world of death, but the reality has nonetheless changed, having passed over into the fullness of Christ. Thus basic structures remain the same in Christians after their baptism, chrismation, marriage, or forgiveness, and yet "a new being is there to see": "for anyone who is in Christ, there is a new creation: the old order is gone" (2 Cor 5:17).

The transfiguration effected in the liturgy is thus a true "passage". By the second operation of his energy the Holy Spirit accomplishes in us the passage of Christ from the present world to the life of the Father. He does not create from nothing, but he does transform: he divinizes. Yes, "he will transfigure the wretched body of ours into the mold of [the] glorious body" of the Lord (Phil 3:21). The cry "May your glory come and this world pass away!"[3] does not mean the annihilation of the world with the kingdom replacing it but the painful gestation of the body of Christ in the womb of the last times. Only death is destroyed, and the fissures caused by sin are filled in. Such is the purpose of grace as a gratuitous initiative and outpouring of the living God in the humanity of the Word. This grace, which was manifested at the first "coming" of the Lord, is deployed in the epiclesis, the heart of the liturgy. It is the agape of the Blessed Trinity, offered to men solely because of the love with which they are loved and not because of their works or merits. It is the purely merciful love that fills the abyss of our wretchedness. It is the Holy Spirit in a state of kenosis: then death disappears, and the body of Christ rises, alive, from our tomb.

In the operation of this energy by which the Spirit makes us become him whom we contemplate there are no determinisms at work, for these would be traces of a death still operative. Grace is free and liberating. It is not conditioned by anything, nor can anything halt it once faith opens itself to it. No closed door can prevent the risen Lord from pouring out his Spirit to "convert" hearts and "convert" everything into his glorious body. The very real transformation that takes place at the heart of the liturgy does not suppose the bringing into play of any created means: it springs up like a new creation. That is why the only thing we can *do* in this synergy with the Holy Spirit is *be* truly ourselves with the accepted truth of our being in relation to the Father, a truth that consists in believing; faith is the free acceptance of the free gift that makes us exist. It is these two freedoms, which reach to depths not touched by the wounds death has inflicted on us, that make the "union" of love possible and

<hr />

[3] *Didache* 10.

allow it to be "transforming". Christ creates in us a desire for the Spirit, and we ask him of the Father; the Father gives us the Spirit of his Son, and we become Christ. Such is the wonderful work of the Spirit who divinizes us in the liturgy as celebrated and experienced: the wellspring creates a thirst in us and slakes that thirst with the Spirit, so that we become the body of Christ.[4]

The Communion of the Body of Christ

Transfiguration is completed in communion, which is a foretaste of the kingdom; it is completed in the "indwelling" of love in which the Three Persons commune with us in oneness. That is doubtless the truth Peter sensed when he suggested raising three tents on the top of the mountain. When men are brought into the Father's dwelling, they already begin to live in communion with him; they anticipate the end and completion of time. But in the liturgy the Church, which is already the communion of those who believe in the name of the beloved Son and have been changed into him, "becomes what it is"; that is, it becomes the body of Christ and a sacrament of the *communion* between God and men.

This body is a living body because the Holy Spirit is communion (2 Cor 13:13). This body is not monolithic but organic, being composed of living members who in turn are endowed with many different charisms by the one Spirit. If the body is a sacrament of communion, then each member

---

[4] See 1 Cor 12:13. Note the nuance of difference between the two Greek prepositions used in this verse (a nuance often missed in modern translations): "baptized *into* one body" ("into" = Greek *eis*, which is dynamic = "in order to form") and "*in* a single Spirit" (*in* = Greek *en*, which is locative).

is likewise a sacrament in his limited way. Christians as such are sacramental beings; in the body they share in the kenosis of love of the Lord and his Spirit. If the first meaning of "communion" is a sharing of the same role with others, then the Church is a communion because she is so much one with Christ that her entire being shares in her Lord's death and Resurrection. That is why only the baptized are agents of the liturgy in the present world. Moreover, through chrismation they have also received the gift of the Spirit as Person, who by his energies enables them to be servants, in the one Servant, of all the epicleses that will be entrusted to them, each according to his or her charisms, both in the liturgy as celebrated and in the liturgy as lived.

The energy of communion that is deployed by the Holy Spirit thus turns the body of Christ into "a kingdom of priests" (1 Pet 2:9), "a kingdom of priests to serve his God and Father" (Rev 1:6). There is only one Priest, "compassionate and trustworthy", "Jesus, the Son of God . . . who has gone through to the highest heaven" (Heb 2:7; 4:14), and his members share in his priesthood for the same mission of salvation and glory. It is they who are to be seen as present at the eternal liturgy under the image of the 144,000 (Rev 7:4), whereas "the huge number, impossible for anyone to count" (vv. 9–17), symbolizes rather the multitude of the elect. The latter are the whole of saved humanity, while the former are the little remnant, the Church, the body of the communion in which the multitude is saved.

Finally, what the Holy Spirit effects in this third energy is expressed in the last symbol of the liturgical vision recounted in the Apocalypse: the trees of life. The image refers us to the communion of the body of Christ. There is in truth but a single tree of life: Christ crucified who gives life. Christians, however, having been crucified with him, rise with him even

now; in him they become a "life-giving spirit". The Spirit
has become in them and with them a single divine energy,
namely, their new being. Death can no longer hobble this
being: they "bear twelve crops of fruit in a year, one in each
month" (Rev 22:2), that is, unceasingly, since they carry within
them the completion of time. "And the leaves . . . are a cure
for the nations": this expresses the entire mission of the Church
in the last times.

The Liturgy, Synergy of the Spirit, and the Church

Two images predominate in the language that the Bible uses
to suggest the mystery of the Church: the image of a body,
which is developed chiefly by Saint Paul, and the image of a
bride, which is to be found more often in Saint John. The
mystery of the liturgy as transfiguration shows, beyond the
images, two coherent symbolisms for the joint mission of
the Word and the Spirit. Insofar as the Church is the body of
Christ, she is one with him; insofar as she is his bride, she is
distinct from him. The union thus involves no confusion.
The Church is a bride, or pure receptivity toward her Lord,
because the Holy Spirit lives in her by his energies, his personal kenosis. Then, being one with the Spirit, the Church
becomes fruitful, bearing the "whole" body of Christ. We
cannot apply deductive reasoning to such symbols. We can
only accept them and by means of them share in the mystery
of the trinitarian communion that was kept hidden through
all the ages and is revealed today in the Church. The source
of that communion for us is the body of Jesus, who is now
risen and living in the Father; the river of life is the Spirit
and the Bride of the Lamb in their mysterious synergy, which
is the liturgy.

In contrast to our various forms of activism that claim to liberate man through every action done on his behalf, the kenosis of the Spirit in the Church reminds us that the liberating event of Christ's Pasch-Passage is simply offered to us in every event and that it must be brought to bear with us and through us. For the Spirit of the risen Christ to be in a state of kenosis means that he is offered, handed over, without any "will to power" and that he requires from us acceptance and response, the same "Yes" of kenosis. This kind of "Yes" on the part of the Virgin allowed the Incarnation of the Word to take place; it was likewise from the consent of the humanity of Jesus that the divinizing light of the transfiguration sprang, and it is the same consent by the Church that allows the liturgy to be celebrated and lived.

We cannot recognize the body of Christ if we forget that we are the Church which conceives that body in faith and carries it toward birth in hope. The routine to which we are prone will reduce the sacraments to "sacred things" if we are not alive to the Spirit who transfigures us through them. For all the energy put forth by the Holy Spirit is experienced at the heart of the Church and in the Church's light-filled humanity, and the Church as such has no energy that is not the energy of her Lord's Spirit. The sacramentality of the Church means that in her everything is the joint energy of the Spirit and of the humanity that he transfigures. This synergy constitutes the liturgy, and it is the liturgy with its threefold process of deification that we are now going to consider in celebration and in life.

PART TWO

THE LITURGY CELEBRATED

After having glimpsed the fontal depths from which the mystery of the liturgy streams forth, we are in a position to receive it in its fullness. The liturgy becomes ours when we celebrate it. Then we drink from the wellspring and can satisfy him who asks us for a drink; in the meeting of these two thirsts the Holy Spirit is the river of life that saves men and makes them bear fruit for the glory of the Father.

The mystery that had been wrapped in silence through everlasting ages and then had been concealed in creation, now journeyed with men and entrusted itself patiently to our fathers in the faith during the time of the promises. Its coming in the fullness of time was made known in the kenosis of the incarnate Word until it became event in the hour of Jesus' Cross and Resurrection. At that point the liturgy streamed forth. In his Ascension Christ celebrates it, eternal and life giving, in the presence of the Father, and pours it out upon the world through the gift of his Spirit: there it effects the coming of the Church and inaugurates the last times. It is the river of life that gushes out from the throne of God and the Lamb; it is a synergy of the Spirit and the Bride, which in the Church conceives, forms, and gives birth to the body of the whole Christ. In the fullness of time *all* of us were in Christ; at the consummation of time he will be *all* in us: the liturgy of the last times is this gestation of the "all" in "all"; it is the transfiguration of the body of Christ.

We must first of all be drawn into the ebb and flow of the liturgy and its celebration. A celebration is an epiphany of the liturgy in the last times (chapter 9), because in its celebration the liturgy spreads abroad (chapter 10). We will then be able to be apprehended by the great sacrament that is the body of Christ (chapter 11). On this basis the irresistible unfolding of the Lord's Ascension will be manifested, that is, the transfiguration of the whole of human life (chapter 12), of time (chapter 13), and of space (chapter 14) through the sacraments.

Chapter 9

The Celebration as Epiphany of the Liturgy

Before seeing how the single event of the liturgy unfolds in its varied celebrations, there is a prior question I must ask: What does it mean to "celebrate" the liturgy? In answering it, I shall be answering another question implicit in the outlook of many Christians: Why celebrate the liturgy?

Celebration as a "Moment" in the Liturgy

A first point has clearly emerged from our contemplation of the mystery as we have glimpsed it in the foregoing chapters: the liturgy is not reducible to the content of our celebrations of it. Christ, in the Holy Spirit and together with "the assembly of the firstborn", is at every moment celebrating the liturgy before the Father. It is this liturgy that shapes history and gives vitality to the Church in our world; it is constantly at work and is offered to us. "Let all who are thirsty come!" (Rev 22:17). Our celebrations are moments in which "all who want it may have the water of life, and have it free" (ibid.). But these moments are not simply moments in the everyday sense, that is, brief segments of time in the day, week, or year. In the economy of salvation they are "moments" in a far richer sense.

In the eschatological "times" in which we are now living, a celebration is a "moment" in the same sense as all other events in the economy of salvation: it, like them, is a special intervention of the living God in human history. The entire economy is punctuated by what the Bible calls *kairoi*, that is, moments of grace, occasions of decision. Our individual lives and those of all men are marked by these reminders in which God urges us to return to him and to encounter him. Our lives thus have "moments" in which the heart is rent and opens itself to the Lord who comes to it. But, as we have seen, the economy turned into liturgy once the river of life leaped forth from the tomb. A celebration can now be seen as a "moment" in which the Lord comes with power and his coming becomes the sole concern of those who answer to his call.

That concern should pervade every other concern of Christian life. Every celebration of the liturgy is geared to that lived liturgy in which each instant of life should become a "moment" of grace. The liturgy cannot be lived at each moment, however, unless it is celebrated at certain moments. Furthermore, the celebration contains an irreducible newness that is an argument for its necessity, for it is in the celebration that the event of Christ becomes the event of the Church assembled here and now. The celebrating Church welcomes the heavenly liturgy and takes part in it. The Church is thereby shown to be the body of Christ and becomes that body more fully, for in the memorial that she celebrates the Spirit feeds her with the Word, transforms it into his body, which is given to her, and extends his communion among the members and with all men. The celebration is thus a fontal moment in which the river of life renews the trees of life and gives them new growth and vitality.

This moment is ecclesial, or it does not exist at all. We saw this to be so at the coming of the Church on Pentecost:

the Spirit gives life to men by making them the body of
Christ. Without moments of celebration the word of God
would be simply an edifying memory, and communion in
love an inaccessible ideal, like an inaccessible fountain before
which we would die of thirst. In short, the epiclesis would
be lacking in which the triple synergy of Spirit and Bride is
established; there would be no event. Without celebration
faith would be once again reduced to theism, hope would
be cut off from its anchor, and charity would be diluted into
a simple love of men. If the Church did not celebrate the
liturgy, she would cease to be the Church and would be no
more than a social body, a residual semblance of the body of
Christ.

The pseudomysticism that rejects celebration of the liturgy is in fact a form of death; the sin of individualism closes
men against the irruption into their lives of the event of the
Resurrection. No person, baptized or not, has a direct line
of communication with the heavenly liturgy. The mystery of
Christ can be "embodied" only in his body; but his "spiritual" body in this world is the Church. Wherever the Church
celebrates the liturgy, there the Spirit of Christ's body is.

Those who claim to live by the risen Christ without the
mediation of the ecclesial celebration of the Resurrection
are involved in a contradiction. How is it possible to live in
communion with the Lord while at the same time living in
isolation and separation from him? How can men go to the
Father while scorning the only way that he has opened to
himself, the way by which he seeks us out and which is coherent with our integral human condition, namely, the body of
his Son? A disincarnate spiritualism has a mistaken idea of
the human person and of God because it ignores the humanity of Christ. But the real humanity of the Lord ever since
his Resurrection is the humanity of Jesus and his members as

a single body in one and the same Spirit. Those who "absent
themselves from the assembly" that celebrates the Lord's Day
(Heb 10:25) have not yet "recognized the body of Christ";
they even introduce division into that body.[1]

The Celebration as Place of the Liturgy

In the name of this same realism it must be said that a celebration is the moment in which *a* Church participates in
the heavenly liturgy. In this intense moment the Lord comes
to his Church that is gathered here in this place. This *local*
participation in the one liturgy reveals to us in turn two further aspects of a celebration.

First, if the Church does the celebrating, she can only be
the Church that is at Corinth or Ephesus or Paris or in some
other place. The Church is thus local or she is not at all. If
the Spirit is poured out upon a community in which the
word dwells in order to transform it into the body of Christ
and extend his communion thereby, this can only occur in a
particular place; otherwise we are dealing with an abstraction. Before being an administrative or pastoral framework,
the idea of "place" that "Church" always connotes sums up
the various elements that sacramentally constitute and structure a particular Church: the baptized-and-confirmed and
their ordained ministers; their language and culture; their

---

[1] The old saying "I'm a believer, but I do not practice" also calls for discernment. From the pastoral point of view, we are dealing here either with
someone who was "prematurely" baptized and is really a catechumen or with
an unwitting penitent. Early Christian liturgical assemblies were familiar
with both categories and provided for their gradual participation in the
eucharistic liturgy. See the successive dismissals of catechumens and penitents
before the anaphora.

living tradition; in short, everything that goes to make a Church the center of the epiclesis that transforms a human community into the body of Christ. In this sense, every celebration is eschatological and in movement toward its consummation, like the Church that celebrates the liturgy.

Second, when a local Church celebrates the liturgy in accordance with the conditions peculiar to her place, she does not celebrate "her own" liturgy as though this were different from the liturgy of the other local Churches. The difference is in the expression, not in the mystery being expressed; always and everywhere it is the same unique heavenly liturgy that is celebrated by all of the local Churches. Because every celebration is a participation in the one heavenly liturgy, it manifests and makes real the catholicity of the Church. This is true especially of the celebration of the eucharistic liturgy. Just as each believer who receives the Body and Blood of Christ receives Christ in his entirety and not simply a part of him, so too the celebration of a local Church does not fragment the heavenly liturgy but participates fully in it. The celebration is thus not only the moment but also the place in which the liturgy gives experience of the Church in the totality of its mystery.

It is through the celebration that all the local Churches manifest, concretize, and communicate their unity in catholicity; all of them participate in one and the same eternal liturgy. In light of this we can see how the manifestation of the mystery of the Church as the eternal liturgy at the heart of history is of fundamental importance for a truthful implementation of all relations in the Church, from the pastoral sphere to ecumenism. This light enables us to eliminate the temptations that periodically trouble the Church, sometimes attracting her to a spiritual corporativism, sometimes to an administrative juridicism. The reason is that at her foundation everything in the Church is liturgy: unity in faith and communion in love, ministries and mission, prayer and the sacred canons. The liturgy is the source.

The Celebration as Center of the Liturgy

The Church's celebration, being the moment and place of the heavenly liturgy, is also the center from which the light of the mystery radiates into the world of the last times. It "focuses" the energies of the transfiguration and applies them to a particular human situation here and now. This center is the point at which the liturgy, which is the Church's deepest life, comes into contact with the incarnate condition of each Church. Now it is noteworthy that all ecclesial celebrations show certain constants, no matter what the particular traditions peculiar to the individual Churches. From the beginning down to our own time the celebration, at its sacramental heart, is structured by permanently constitutive elements. Whether the celebration be of a vigil office or the reconciliation of penitents, the anointing of the sick or the Eucharist, a kind of common morphology seems to emerge from all the varied ecclesial celebrations.[2]

First of all, there is an *assembly*, however small, of the baptized-and-confirmed; otherwise the body of Christ would not be signified, and the celebration would not be a celebration of the liturgy. There are also *ministers*, at least one of whom must have been ordained for this service; otherwise, the Spirit and the Bride would not be signified, Christ would not be the servant of his body, and the assembly might perform

[2] "Ecclesial" distinguishes the liturgy proper from subliturgical gatherings for worship.

an act of religious worship, but it would not be celebrating the Eucharist. The reason why an ordained minister is needed can be readily surmised: the Communion of the Blessed Trinity, which is the ultimate energy at work in the liturgy, is not something men take for themselves but something they receive. Whatever the faithful may think, they do not "give" peace during the celebration; rather they receive it from him who alone is our peace and who gives it within his body and through members ordained for this ministry.[3] In the celebration, those who thirst draw near and "receive" the water of life as a free gift and not by their own powers. When we go deeply enough into the question of ministries we find once again the mystery, so alien to carnal men, of the synergy of the Spirit and the Bride, the mystery of the incarnational realism of the body of Christ and of salvation as an utterly unmerited gift. It is not enough simply that "two or three gather in his name" for Christ to celebrate the liturgy with them.[4]

Another constant is "the word of God", which is proclaimed by a minister and heard by the assembly, meditated on by each individual and kept in the heart. It is because of this that a celebration is a new Pentecost: the Spirit is poured

---

[3] It is not my task here to discuss in detail the very topical question of ministries. The key point is that according to the tradition of the apostolic Churches, ordained ministers are essentially at the service of the sacramental epiclesis; this is the criterion by which to judge their other functions and the distinction of these from the analogous functions (e.g., proclamation of the word) of the royal priesthood.

[4] Mt 18:19–20. The Lord is in the midst of the "two or three". If they are united (but do they know whether they are?), the Father hears their petition. In this case, however, it is not yet the Church but simply a community of believers that awaits the new Pentecost. Most important of all, their activity is not a celebration, since the body of Christ is organic and not anarchic: the Spirit makes us part of this body; we do not construct it. See 1 Cor 12:12–14.

out on those in whom the word dwells; he "reminds" them of it so that he may enable them to experience the event that is the word and may "lead" them "to the complete truth". But a celebration is not a course on the Bible or a sharing of the impressions each person derives from the word. In a celebration the Christ event becomes the event of the Church and is therefore a moment in holy, living tradition; the heart of Jerusalem is made fruitful by the river of life, and the hungry receive the bread of the word from the apostles who distribute it to them. The word of God, present at the heart of the celebration, must be refracted in the body; there it becomes *the word of the Church*. It is not my subjective words that make me a member of the assembly, much less a minister of the word, but the Word of life, whose body is the Church. Apart from this body there can be many spirits, but not the Spirit of Christ, who speaks through the prophets.

A further constant of which a certain type of person who is more cerebral than integrally human needs to be reminded is *symbolic actions*. In order for the celebration to effect a transfiguration of the body of Christ, it must involve the whole person, who is a "body". If the light of Tabor touches men at the level of the "heart", that is, the innermost core of freedom that has been delivered from structures, it is in order that their entire being may be enlightened and divinized. A cerebral celebration inevitably leads by way of compensation to intellectual or emotional self-satisfaction. In contrast, an integral celebration of the liturgy leads the participant to the center of faith and finds expression in communion, both of the individual and of the community. The Christ event becomes the event of his Church only if it is acted out and not simply thought or felt. Thought and feeling create idols; only symbols in action lead into the mystery. This participation in the mystery is then expressed by the faith of the assembly; this is the significance of *song*: not a cacaphonous juxtaposition of spoken words but a harmonious unity in faith, intercession, and doxology. This is a further register or level of the Church's word, but it signifies in this case an effective participation in the Christ event and a communion in faith.

The structural constants of the celebration include, finally, a certain *space* and a certain *time*.[5] When we say "space" and "time" we think immediately of the functional aspect of these realities, and this is valid enough; but they have a much deeper meaning than that. After all, it is the very newness of the risen Christ himself that is trying to make its way through to us in the celebration. "Closed doors" are no longer barriers to his presence, and time is no longer swallowed up in the past, because Jesus in his person is our "today". If the eternal liturgy unfolds in our world and in our time in the form of the Lord's Ascension, this fact ought to be signified at the heart of the celebration. I am not thinking of some kind of pyschedelic conditioning of the congregation or of a theater of illusion. The point is rather that in the sacramental realism of the body of Christ, space and time ought to be expressed as transfigured. In our human celebrations of anniversaries or victories, we spontaneously find signs that make it possible for space and time to share in the event being celebrated. Why then should we overlook this incarnational and very human dimension in the celebration of the liturgy, the event that sustains and transfigures everything? Here, of course, the light comes from within, and if it is lacking, we regress into cultic folklore. Throughout the history of the Church the local Churches have found widely differing ways of expressing space and time, probably because these two

[5] See chaps. 13 and 14.

aspects of a celebration are the ones most closely bound up with contingent cultures; in the present-day change that is occurring in civilizations we cannot forget these same two aspects without beclouding this central reality—the celebration—through which the liturgy unfolds in the Church and influences the world.

These eight constants (to which others could be added depending on the traditions proper to the various Churches) give every celebration its structure. They are not deduced from a logic of ritual but are simply observable in and inferred from the universal practice of the Churches. As a matter of fact, they demonstrate the sacramental condition proper to the liturgy in the last times. For in them we find the prime coordinates of all communication among persons: group, word, gesture, space, and time. Here, however, they are used by Christ the Lord to channel the floodtide of his Spirit. For the Word's assumption of what is human is wholly ordered to the Pentecost that is effected by the epiclesis in the celebration. That is why these various constants have an entirely different significance here than they do in an assembly that is analyzable in purely sociological terms. Not only do we find two original and irreducible elements—the word of God that is communicated through Scripture and its proclamation, and ministries that are energies of the Spirit—but these two signs and the other six would cease utterly to signify the liturgy if we were to reduce them to the meaning the participants would like them to have. They are signs only because the mystery transfigures them from within; then they serve to lead us into the liturgy. If this were not the case, we would be back in the sacred ritual of the natural religions or the various ideologies.

The celebration is not only the time, place, and center of the liturgy but also its epiphany, since it allows it to radiate out in various energies. Thus while all celebrations show a basic likeness in the signs that manifest the mystery, they differ significantly in the energies of the Holy Spirit that effectively communicate this mystery. All of them celebrate the coming of the Lord, but not all do so with the same power. The transforming energy exercised by the Spirit through the common structural signs differs depending on the celebration. Since there is but one sacrament, namely, the body of Christ that is the Church, every celebration participates in it and gives a participation in it; but there is a variety of energies of the Holy Spirit to meet the different needs of man who is to be divinized, and therefore there is a variety of celebrations.

To put it plainly, the living tradition of the apostolic Churches enables us to experience the liturgy first of all in the celebration of the great sacrament—the Divine Liturgy par excellence, the Eucharist—which cannot be put on the same level as any other celebration because it contains the whole of the mystery. It is the total "moment" of both the local Church and the communion of Churches. The liturgy is experienced, next, in the major sacraments: baptism and chrismation, reconciliation of penitents and anointing of the sick, marriage and the ordination of ministers. But within these sacramental energies there are other "signs" by which the Lord manifests and communicates his glory, especially the Bible and the icon,[6] the Lord's Day and the other "significant moments" of transfigured time.

At this point a seemingly naive question deserves an answer. It is a question sometimes asked by those who are just beginning to encounter the risen Christ: Why this variety of litur-

---

[6] The complementarity of Bible and icon as written forms of the one economy of salvation was defined at the Seventh Ecumenical Council (Nicea II, in 787).

gical celebration? Since Christ is in our midst, why does not the energy of the Spirit manifest itself through a single sign? Is it possible for the life-giving action of the risen Christ to be "more" and "less"?

A first answer is given by a fact: the Eucharist and the major sacraments come to us from Christ and the first apostolic community. They are facts of tradition; the liturgy is not invented but received. These great sacraments are "covenant signs", seals upon fidelity, "moments" of union, which the Lord gives and entrusts to his Bride in his Spirit. Other forms of celebration are contingent, although inasmuch as all the local Churches have gradually adopted them in the course of history, even our critical approach (itself needing to be criticized) can hardly reject them out of hand. In the liturgy creativity is also an energy of the Spirit working at the heart of the Church, and it is authentic as long as the touchstone is the mystery of Christ.

A second answer also appeals to a fact of tradition and to the continuity between the economy and the liturgy. Before his Resurrection Christ acted toward his fellow man with the simplicity and truthfulness of a living person. Now that Christ, our God, "has passed over into his mysteries", he is even more "human" than he was during his mortal life. In human communication, however, presence has a whole range of expressions: word, gesture, silence, look, writing, and so on. In each of these forms it is always ourselves whom we communicate, but our "presence" is not the same without distinction in all of them. In the relationship of the Lord to his Church and to each member of his body the gift of his presence has an even more nuanced range of expressions. First, there is the sacrament of his body, in which his presence is total because his Passage contains everything; then there are the other sacraments or, better, sacramental energies, which respond with surprising fidelity to our human thirst and all the forms of the human desire for God.

In the final analysis, there is a great variety of celebrations because the liturgy is no less pedagogically oriented than the economy that it fulfills. In this mystery of Covenant the Spouse is not always as wide awake and present as "he who handed himself over for her" might expect. The nuances in the sacramental scale show forth this hidden pedagogy of the Spirit. Thus a penitential celebration in the form of a "liturgy of the word" is not yet a celebration of the sacrament of conversion with its crowning epiclesis, but it prepares the way for the latter; and when reconciliation is lived out in the eucharistic liturgy the energy of communion goes even further, while always presupposing conversion. It is clear that while discernment or recognition of the body of Christ is presupposed by every celebration, each celebration with its pedagogical originality enables us to recognize how "many sided" the wisdom of the Lord's Spirit is (Eph 3:10). His energies are multiform, and the sacraments that celebrate them are "for us men". The entire economy of salvation that flows into the liturgy is a plan marked by "condescension", because the Spirit has accustomed himself to dwelling with men.[7]

Celebration as Feast of the Liturgy

There is one word that sums up the mystery of celebration as epiphany of the liturgy: feast. The verb "celebrate", which

---

[7] In the Bible and the Fathers of the Church the word "condescension" (Greek: *synkatabasis*) does not signify a patronizing attitude, as it does in English. It suggests rather the tender love of the Father as he bends down to his children in order to be with them; it also expresses the first movement of the Pasch/Passage (the second being the Ascension), which is followed now by the outpouring of the Holy Spirit. See Bar 3:38; Prov 8:31; Jn 1:14.

today has at last replaced the "say" (Mass, Office) and "per-form" (baptisms, for example) of decadent ages, already ori-ents us to the experience of feast; the purpose is not to "hold" a feast once again or to "give vent" to our unconscious impulses, but to participate in the feast of the eternal liturgy. Before pulling the strings for stage settings that might help to provide a festive ambiance, this is the time, if ever there was one, for getting back to the source, the wellspring. To celebrate the liturgy is to enter into the joy of the Father, the only joy that can enable us to share Christ's exultation in the Holy Spirit (Lk 10:21). True enough, festivity has its origin in an event that makes us happy; but do we realize that the good news, the happy news, here is that we are to be cru-cified with Jesus in order to rise with him? A feast celebrates an encounter, but to whom does the Spirit lead the Bride in the celebration? To celebrate an event with a feast is to enable others to share our joy, but how is a celebration such as the anointing of the sick or the forgiving of my sins truly such a sharing and an anticipation of the kingdom? Each of us can add to these questions and enter more fully into the inex-haustible newness of the feast to which we are given access in every celebration.

When viewed in the light of the mystery of the heavenly liturgy,[8] our festive celebrations make two demands of us. The first demand is for faith and conversion, because a cel-ebration is a moment of intensity in the coming of the Lord. The two levels of which the Apocalypse speaks to us—the drama of history and the eternal liturgy—can be glimpsed as present in the celebration. This should be dazzlingly clear to our faith, even when everything in us, except our heart, is in darkness. Our hands touch the wounds of the crucified

[8] See chap. 4.

Servant, and our hearts acknowledge him as the Lord our God. But we do not attain to this simple faith by the mere act of entering a church and beginning a celebration. Here again a path, a sequence of steps, is needed. This is why the liturgical tradition and its pedagogy always have us begin with adoration and acknowledgment of our sins before we listen to the Word and participate in his saving event. We approach the burning bush in the liturgy only after we have removed our shoes and prostrated ourselves.

The second demand has to do with the authenticity of our lives. How can we be filled with jubilant wonder and thanksgiving in our celebrations—including those for the dead—if the power of the Resurrection does not daily penetrate the depths of our sinfulness and death? How can we share the Father's joy if we are not constantly open to his overwhelming mercy? How can we sing the canticle of the Lamb, the canticle sung by the blood of the martyrs and the perseverance of the saints, if we do not pray for our oppressors? And since the only true joy is paschal joy, joy in the life that springs from the victory over death, how can we celebrate the feast that is the liturgy if we have not learned to be "glad of . . . distress for Christ's sake" (2 Cor 12:10) in the details of our everyday lives, as the Father takes delight in his beloved Son (Mt 17:5)? In short, how can we celebrate the liturgy if we do not live it? The converse is also true: we can live it only if we celebrate it, as we shall see in the third part of this book.

In this ebb and flow of the river of life that springs from the Father and returns to him in Christ, the "moments" constituted by our celebrations are thus manifestations of the liturgy. There are also its ever new outpourings in us and with us.

Chapter 10

The Outstreaming of the Liturgy
in the Celebration

In our effort to understand how the Church celebrates the liturgy, we have drawn near to the moment, the place, the very center at which the everlasting feast of the Pasch bursts through into our time of groans and tears, and we have seen the celebration to be the manifestation or epiphany of the liturgy. It is time now to inquire how the river of life can thus be so close to our lips in the celebration that from it we can drink the water that satisfies our desire. How does the liturgy as manifested in the celebration give us life? How does the synergy of the Spirit and the Bride act in the sacraments being celebrated so that we experience the transfiguration of the body of Christ?

In fostering the effort to recognize the body of Christ I shall first be careful to point out the impasses into which we are led astray by interpretations of the liturgy that forget the wellspring of living water; these are our cracked water tanks (Jer 2:13). I shall then be better able to show how during the exodus, which the people of God is accomplishing in the last times, the Lord is active at the heart of the celebration, where he splits the rock and out streams the water (Is 48:21). Then, as the search for the meaning of the celebration continues, the various ways or "methods" [1]

[1] Etymologically, "method" means "traveling with", accompanying.

by which God leads us to the springs of water (Is 49:10) will reveal themselves.

Cracked Water Tanks

Despite their bare simplicity, our sacramental celebrations are made up of rather complex elements, as we have already seen.[2] If we want to understand what we are experiencing at these "moments" of the liturgy, we must travel the way of these elements, for we realize that they are signs and thus consistent with the entire economy of the Incarnation. But these realistic sacramental signs also call for a strict discernment by faith. As we look for living water, do we not tend to forget the wellspring and to dig our own cisterns? The temptation is obvious. After all, the eight constitutive elements or constants that make up the heart of the celebration—assembly and ministers, word of God read in the Bible and words of the Church that we speak, symbolic actions and song, space and time—form a set of signs that we can control; we can understand them along a particular line and mold and adjust them. Meanwhile, the wellspring. . . . Christians have been chronically tempted since the beginning of the Church's existence to make the liturgy fit a mold that is "intelligible", only to find, too late, that the mold contains nothing but what they themselves have put into it: a desperate thirst. We are in a position today to detect three forms of this temptation.

The first form is *cultural*. It consists in listing the visible and tangible components of celebrations and then interpreting them in the light of cultural criteria. The drawback here is not the attempt as such but its myopic character. In Chris-

---

[2] Chap. 9.

tian antiquity two explanatory models predominated, and their influence reached down into the Middle Ages. Following the lead of Aristotle, some thinkers studied the sacraments in terms of their substantial and accidental, formal and material makeup; their efficacy, though seen as dependent on the Church, was conceived primarily in terms of causality. Following the lead of Plato and Plotinus, other thinkers were more alert to the meaning of the sacraments and to their symbolism with its reference to the nonmaterial world; their efficacy was expressed in terms rather of participation. In our time, these two intellectual approaches have been tested in the crucible of the changes in thinking—sometimes more materialistic, sometimes more idealistic—of the past century and have been enriched by the contributions of psychology and sociology and by all the discoveries of hermeneutics.

All these various approaches, which are fascinating in their own way and not without pastoral consequences, focused on the sacramental signs and led to something signified that was accessible to the microscope employed by each discipline. The list of a cistern's contents is not without its interest, but what about the source, the wellspring? As long as one does not take the wellspring as the point of departure, one cannot receive its living water. Failure to take the wellspring into account leads to a view of the sacraments as petrified efficacious signs—but efficacious of what? "Of grace"— but what is this grace? Divine helps, or even participation in the life of God? But Plotinus said that much! And why the need to pass through these signs and thus through the lowliness of the flesh?

It will never be possible in any cultural interpretation to bring in the mystery of Christ as we saw it in the first part of the present book. The realism of the event of the Resurrection, the paradox of the last times, the synergy of the Spirit and the Church, the body of Christ and its transfiguration, the whole newness of Christ—all these become a mirage in these various forms of horizontalism, even if the latter be still inspired by a theistic faith. Only the fontal liturgy can transfigure the sacraments as signs and enable us to experience them as synergies at work in the body of Christ, the one Sacrament.

The second form is that displayed by fundamentalist believers who cling to the letter of the Bible; this is the *cultic* temptation. These people prefer the term "worship", because the word "liturgy" suggests nothing to them.[3] The word "sacrament", for its part, has been so reified by a decadent Scholasticism that fundamentalists are rather reserved toward its use.[4] Furthermore, the model they use in interpreting Christian cult is unconsciously inspired by the Old Testament. In the latter, there were saving events; these were memorialized in worship, while the moral life had to conform to the laws revealed in all the events that were celebrated in worship. The human mind is comfortable with this tripartite division familiar from the catechism: truths to be believed, commandments to be kept, means of sanctification. All the monotheisms have it in common. So do the ideocracies.

Fortunately, the mystery of Christ is no longer present. In worship in spirit and truth the saving event, the liturgy, and the new life all meet and become one. Because the event of the Cross and Resurrection is always life giving here and now, ritualism is overcome: a sacred sign and the event it signifies

---

[3] Only in one passage (Acts 13:2) does the New Testament use the word "liturgy" as a synonym for Christian worship; on all other occasions it refers to the new life of Christians. Furthermore, we will look in vain in the canonical apostolic writings for any "order" for a liturgical celebration.

[4] Even in the case of marriage, despite Saint Paul's clear statement in Eph 5:32.

are no longer separated. The sacred is not identifiable with
the sacramental, for it is the body of Christ that is *the* sacrament. As a result, moralism too is overcome: there is no longer an exteriority, a heteronomy of the law in relation to
Christian action, because the Spirit of the body of Christ
becomes our life. The newness of Christ makes available to
us the wellspring, the liturgy; when the latter is celebrated,
the paschal event from which it leaps forth becomes our life.

There is left the perhaps more recent and certainly more
seductive third form of the basic temptation: *everything is now
sacramental*. We might use a learned word and describe it as
"omnisacramentalism". It is seemingly valid because it has
latched on to an intoxicating truth: that the risen Christ is
now present and acting in all things. From this it follows
(they say) that everything is transfigured and becomes a sign
pregnant with his presence. As a result, all, according to their
tastes, can find sacraments everywhere: our brother is a sacrament, as are nature, art and culture, guerillas, the mainte-
nance of order, psychoanalysis, group dynamics, and so on.
The age of the sacramental panacea has dawned, and wildcat
celebrations proliferate.

This sudden high temperature is perhaps an indication of
a crisis of growth. In any case, it calls for increased discernment. In addition to fostering the subjectivist illusion that
the liturgy can be lived without being celebrated in the body
from which it emerges, this angelic interpretation fails to
acknowledge an elementary fact about the last times: while
we are "already" all in Christ, he is "not yet" all in all; everything subsists in him, but this world is still in the power of
the evil one. Religious pietism is always the revenge taken
by doctrinal idealism. The merit of this neopietism is its keen
sense that anything and everything can become an epiphany
of the risen Lord. On the other hand, it leads to an impasse

to the extent that it fails to recognize the only road leading to this transfiguration, namely, the event of the Cross and Resurrection as offered and accepted in the celebration of the liturgy.

"He Split the Rock and Out Streamed the Water" (Is 48:21)

How, then, does the liturgy that manifests itself in the celebration give us life? We cannot take the liturgical signs as our sole starting point and conclude to an unknown signified; this is the approach taken by the various forms of religious ritualism, and it leads us astray. We must move rather from the mystery as revealed to us in the economy of salvation to its concretization in the liturgy. This is the course I have been following since the beginning of the present book. When the signs split open they become transparent, and the water can stream out. This clarified vision that first reaches to the mystery and then, from within, sheds light on its signs is the vision of faith. It is in the meeting of two freedoms—that of faith and that of the Spirit—that the transfiguration, that is, the sacramental liturgy, is experienced. It is not possible from that point on to think of the sacraments in terms of sacred things or causalities or participation or signifiers to be decoded. They can be thought of only in terms of life: the life of God living in our flesh and the life of our humanity living in the Word; and in terms even of energies, since the focus here is on the event that is to become real and active. To put it better: one can slake one's thirst at the living, streaming water only if one experiences the astonishing synergy of the Spirit and the Church. The whole mystery of the sacraments resides in this synergy.

Nicholas Cabasilas tells us that "the sacraments are the masterpieces of creation". This is not a pious exaggeration. The first creation, which exists only through the kenosis of the living God, began to acquire its meaning during the long period of the promises; the seed of the Word was silently germinating in the faith of the people of God. When the fullness of time came, the entry of the Word in person into our flesh began the upthrust of creation toward its future deliverance. It was no longer opaque, but neither was it transfigured; rather it was beginning to become a parable of the "coming" kingdom, because the kingdom was coming within it. But when the hour of Jesus came, the streaming out of the liturgy and its spread through the last times due to the outpouring of the Holy Spirit marked the coming of the new creation, of which the Church is the firstfruits. This is not a creation *stuck on to* the first creation, or first creation itself *after* the rough-draft stage; rather it is the body of Christ *in* and *with* our first creation. "With" and "in" are stammering efforts to express the synergy of the New Covenant: his dwelling with us; he is in us and we in him. When his life-giving energy meets ours, when these two gratuitous freedoms become one, when the signs of his Covenant are recognized by our faith and welcomed into our flesh, then creation becomes that which it was called to be. That is, it becomes the synergy, the masterpiece of construction, the keystone of the Church of the Ascension, wherein everything is recapitulated in Christ.

We are invited to this continual synergy at every moment, and it is for this that expectant creation "is waiting with eagerness" (Rom 8:19). But let us be honest. On the one hand, in everyday life our gratuitous self-giving and our freedom are half-asleep and, on the other, the "signs", that is, the circumstances of the events in which we find ourselves, are hardly transparent windows through which the Lord is directly seen. But from the beginning and through the entire course of the intense "moment" that is the celebration of a sacrament, the antecedent energy of the Spirit constantly awakens a response of faith in us.[5] As for the sacramental "signs", their sobriety is the best condition for their letting the mystery shine through and for making it visible to our receptive faith.[6]

This sobriety both of the signs and of faith during the celebration is something that needs to be emphasized. It corresponds in a most fitting way to the kenosis that the Holy Spirit experiences in the sacramental synergy. This element of kenosis is, of course, utterly unsuspected by human minds that fall short of faith; it is nonetheless essential to our experience of the sacraments of faith. It is here above all that the sacraments show themselves to be the masterpieces of creation. Everything becomes clear once we realize that creation is not an effect produced by a first cause or a series of emanations from the one into the many (a work, therefore, of the God of the philosophers and the learned), but the first kenosis of the love in the Holy Trinity. Yes, the first creation is so marvelous that neither poetry nor science can grasp it completely. The saving events during the period of the promises were no less spectacular, even if we must sometimes tone down the lyric fervor proper to the epic genre in which they are reported to us. As for the "works" of Jesus during his mortal life, they were astounding to the point of arousing

---

[5] This is the purpose of the liturgy of the word in every sacrament and, more generally, of the word as proclaimed and accepted from the beginning to the end of the celebration.

[6] In the context of a celebration, water, for example, or bread or wine or oil or the imposition of hands can hardly have a meaning except in light of the mystery of faith.

wonder and leading to faith: no one had ever spoken like this man or worked such miracles. At that time, the "signs" were dazzling.

But when the hour comes for the new creation to arise, all this disappears and is replaced by a laughable failure: the folly and weakness of the Cross. What about now, in our last times? The sacraments in which the "wonderful works" of God in the Old Testament and the miracles of Jesus' ministry are brought to fulfillment are manifested in signs so simple that even believers pass them by with indifference. "Truly, you are a God who conceals himself" (Is 45: 15): the closer his return, the thicker the cloud. This kenosis of the Word and of the Holy Spirit, which also affects the Church, is perhaps the most overwhelming revelation of the Father. In the celebration of the sacraments, just as in our life in the Spirit, there is an inverse proportion between spectacle and authenticity, between appearance and effectiveness. In his masterpieces the Father uses a minimum of show and a maximum of omnipotence: "He is, and he is coming." The more radical the kenosis of the Word and the Spirit in the Church—and the sacraments are the time and place of this supreme kenosis—the more the Father disappears from sight. But in that measure he is all the more the Father and the wellspring.

Far from leading to a cerebral stripping away of the signs, the mystery of God's kenosis in the sacraments urges us on the contrary to make our signs authentic and to respond in faith: only through this synergy does a sacrament exist. The humanity of Christ's body, which we are, must be humanly authentic in a way only the Spirit of the Lord can make possible. The Father's compassion never dwells in us so intensely as when we consent to experience the Passion of his Son in the emptiness of our death. The rock that is split at that moment is the tomb, and from it living water streams out. In the celebration of the sacraments we are not onlookers at sacred signs, but must incorporate them into ourselves so that they will express in the fullest possible way "the life that I am now living, subject to the limitation of human nature ... in faith, faith in the Son of God who loved me and gave himself for me" (Gal 2:20).

Living water then streams out, and the synergy of the Spirit and the Church becomes ours. It is of this that the following chapters will be speaking. For the moment, let me simply point out three constants that mark the operation of this synergy in our celebration of the sacraments.

1. First there is the *radical movement* of every celebration. In the hidden depths of the celebration the Father gives himself through his Son in his Holy Spirit; the entire economy attests to this. But in the celebration that was begun at the Ascension the movement of return—the movement of the passage from this world to the Father, the movement proper to a feast—also manifests itself and is operative; the dynamism of the liturgy draws us to the Father through Christ in the Holy Spirit. The river of life that rises from the throne of God and the Lamb then begins to flow back to him in the celebrating Church. To the Father, through the Son, in the Spirit: such was the doxology common to all the Churches in the early centuries. The economy shows us the first movement in the great Passover of history; the liturgy enables us to experience its fulfillment. But this doxology that is the underlying force in every celebration is at the same "moment" a synergy of redemption; it is "soteriological". The body of Christ is inseparably the sacrament both of God's glory and of human salvation. "God's glory is the living man, but the life of men is the vision of God" (Saint Irenaeus). The synergy that streams from every cel-

ebration is a "praise of the glory of his grace" (Eph 1:6) and a divinization of man, a "recapitulation" of all things in Christ (Eph 1:10).

2. There is also (I simply mention the fact once again[7]) the streaming forth of the threefold synergy of the Spirit and the Bride. It impresses *its overall rhythm* on every celebration; through it we reach, in all the sacraments, the fontal liturgy. We are no longer concerned here with the basic structure of a celebration (the eight elements or factors that we studied earlier belong to the world of signs), but are now at the level of what the signs signify and what streams out of them. The three main phases of a sacrament are, first, that in which the Spirit manifests Christ and which we today call "the liturgy of the word"; second, that in which the Spirit transforms, in Christ, what the Church offers to him (the epiclesis that operates at the heart of every sacrament); and, third, the synergy of communion in which Christ is communicated and which overflows into the lived liturgy.

3. The third constant has to do not with the overall rhythm of a celebration but with its *subordinate rhythms*, its lesser stages. I am not saying that in our liturgical *ordines* as they now exist every detail follows a vital logic. There are times when we can legitimately ask why this particular action is done at this point or why that particular thing is said at that other point. Lazy abridgments and decadent additions are not part of the holy tradition, and the patient work of specialists is required to distinguish the authentic from the apocryphal. But to the extent that this kind of purification is effected by the Churches concerned, we can see a progression appear within each of the three main phases of our celebrations; these subordinate rhythms are as it were "sacramental units".

[7] See chap. 8.

A sacramental unit is a harmonious combination of three elements, which of themselves ought to be inseparable: action, word, song.[8] I mention them, not simply because of their structural and significative importance but because of the synergies that they embody. For what is an action in a celebration but a symbol through which the Spirit, together with the Church, effects what is signified? Standing and kneeling, for example, are not simply functional gestures but signify a synergy: the prayer of the risen Jesus and the prayer of the sinner. Furthermore, an action without words quickly becomes ritualistic or magical: it is words that give meaning to an action and awaken the faith that can then be signified. Finally, singing alone enables the assembly to participate in that which it does, understands, and says. In a sacramental unit we also find the threefold energy of the Spirit to which the Church responds: manifestation through the word, fulfillment through action, communion through song. It is the progression of its sacramental units, within the overall rhythm, that constitutes the course of a celebration. This vital logic cannot be deduced from anything else, but it can be verified in pastoral practice. Examination at that level shows that the unjustified absence of one of the three elements in these basic rhythms disturbs the celebration and obscures its meaning.

---

[8] Without venturing on any description of details, which may vary from one ecclesial tradition to another, I cite as examples of sacramental units in the eucharistic liturgy: the three processions (gospel, offertory, Communion), the various moments in the giving of the Pax (peace), the pleas for forgiveness, the various forms of adoration (of the Blessed Trinity or the Body of Christ), the epiclesis, the intercessions, the Our Father, the elevation of the Bread of life and the chalice, the Communion, the blessings that open or close the stages of the celebration.

"He Will Guide Them to Springs of Water" (Is 49:10)

This search for the meaning of our celebrations is extremely important, for it controls our discovery of the meaning of the liturgy in our lives. If we do not find the meaning of our celebrations, they risk becoming moments that are increasingly meaningless and unrelated to life. It seems that from the very beginning of the Church's existence the main concern was the transformation of the Christian's life into the liturgy of the New Covenant. The New Testament writings say very little about celebrations; what interests them is the meaning of the liturgy in our new life.[9] The same holds for the liturgical writings of the early centuries, even though they are also priceless witnesses to the earliest expressions and structures of the celebrated liturgy. But it was especially from the fourth century on that patristic literature acquired a new literary genre devoted to the search for the meaning of liturgical celebrations; I am referring to the mystagogies.[10]

From the Fathers down to our own time it is possible to distinguish four mystagogical methods that differ because of their viewpoint. The first may be called "point oriented"; that is, it takes the moments of a celebration one by one and explains their meaning.[11] In the final analysis, this method

[9] See S. Lyonnet, "La nature du culte dans le Nouveau Testament", in *La Liturgie après Vatican II* (Paris: Cerf, 1967), 357–84.

[10] "Mystagogy" means, literally, "the action of leading to the mystery" or "the action by which the mystery leads us". The principal Fathers who composed mystagogies were Cyril of Jerusalem, John Chrysostom, Theodore of Mopsuestia, Narsai, Pseudo-Dionysius, and Maximus the Confessor.

[11] For example, Nicholas Cabasilas, *A Commentary on the Divine Liturgy*, trans. J. M. Hussey and P. A. McNulty (London: S.P.C.K., 1960), and P. Le Brun, *Explication de la Messe* (Lex orandi 9; Paris: Cerf, 1983).

follows the course of a celebration by looking at its "sacramental units". This kind of catechesis in the Fathers and their successors confirms what I said about the internal rhythm—action, word, song—of these units. This kind of discovery of meaning is inexhaustible.

The second mystagogical method may be called "linear", in the sense that it focuses on the main lines and units of a celebration, in order to bring out its overall, coherent meaning. It is in this method that the overall movement given by the threefold synergy of the Spirit and the Church emerges with full clarity.

A third method is more theological and synthetic and may be called "panoramic". It takes a sacrament and, using it as a center of reference, goes into all aspects of the Christian mystery. Of all the sacraments, the Eucharist doubtless lends itself best to this more systematic mystagogy.[12]

Finally, there is another possible method, though it has been little used by the Fathers and the catechetical instructors of later centuries. It consists in searching out the meaning of a celebration on the basis of the meaning of its uniquely special epiclesis. Here the viewpoint is that of the power of the Resurrection as operative in this sacrament. The meaning sought is the meaning of the energy of the Spirit as it transforms the men offered to it. Such a mystagogy can evidently be fruitful in bringing out the unity of celebration and life, since it is the epiclesis operative in the sacrament that goes on to dynamize the lives of those who have celebrated it.

This fourth way is the one that I shall chiefly follow, using it convergently with the "linear" mystagogy of the

---

[12] The Eucharist is the keystone in the mystagogy of Saint Maximus the Confessor.

threefold synergy. I shall not limit myself to the liturgical expressions peculiar to one or other Church, but shall try to bring out the meaning of the action of the Holy Spirit in those celebrations that are the common treasure of all the apostolic Churches. A mystagogy based on the epicleses can bring out the profound unity of the liturgy as grasped by a simple faith: manifested in glory, celebrated in the flesh, lived in the Spirit.

Chapter 11

The Sacrament of Sacraments

The Eucharist is "the sacrament of sacraments" in which the body of Christ brings to bear all the energies contained in his transfiguration and "accomplishes" his mystery in the Church.[1] It is in him that we assemble on the Lord's day to experience his passage in intense faith and festive joy. In him the Father gives us to share in his communion in the eternal liturgy. But in this celebration of ours the Holy Spirit is the principal "liturgist". It is he who enables us to experience the Eucharist as the mysterious symphony of the incarnate Word; through the Spirit everything that lives and breathes is gathered together in the unity of the Son and sings of the Father's joy.

In a *prelude*, as it were, the Spirit first opens us to the liturgy that is to be celebrated. In the first movement, which is the *liturgy of the word*, he shows us the Lord who is coming. In the second, which is the *anaphora*, he makes the passage of Christ real for us and operative in us. This transformation is completed in the third movement, which is our *communion* in the body of Christ. Then, as in a *finale* in which everything begins anew, he opens us to the liturgy that we are to live out.

[1] Etymologically "celebrate" means "to accomplish". The expression "sacrament of sacraments" is from Pseudo-Dionysius (the reader will recognize "sacrament of sacraments" as the Semitic form of the superlative: the greatest sacrament).

But our liturgist does not accomplish this great Passover of history without our cooperation; we must prepare ourselves for it and respond to it. The celebration is a constant synergy between him and us. That is why at the heart of each of the movements making up the eucharistic liturgy we join him in a kind of two-step rhythm: the awakening of our faith and the faith event. The Spirit opens our eyes in order that we may recognize the Lord; he gathers up our hearts so that they may receive the Word; he intensifies our hunger so that we may be filled with the Bread of Life; he makes us die to ourselves so that we may rise with Christ; he becomes our joy so that we may become the Father's joy; he breathes through us so that we may give life to our brothers and sisters.

These awakenings of our faith make us more and more transparent for the light of the transfiguration to shine through.[2] By his threefold influence the Holy Spirit permeates our being and makes us experience Christ, our Passover. He reveals him to us, actualizes him for us, and makes us participate in him. In each of these three movements there is an especially intense moment in which the Spirit divinizes us in the body of the Lord; that moment is the epiclesis.[3] The liturgy of the word culminates in an epiclesis that precedes the proclamation of the Gospel, for it is in the Gospel that the incarnate Word becomes "spirit and life" for us (see Jn 6:63). In the anaphora the anamnesis has consecratory power, thanks to the epiclesis, in which the Spirit transforms the offerings into the Body and Blood of Christ. In the liturgy of communion it is again by an epiclesis that the bread mingled with the wine in the chalice effects our transformation, the transforming union of the Church with her Lord.

[2] See chap. 7.
[3] See chap. 8.

The Liturgy of the Word

In the economy of the mystery as in its liturgy, the first movement is the movement of love by which the Father gives us his
Word. Therefore, the awakening of faith within us by the Holy
Spirit consists first of all in waiting for the Lord, preparing the
way for him in our hearts, recollecting ourselves in the likeness of him who is coming. Each liturgical tradition gives
expression to these preparatory acts in accordance with its own
pedagogical method.[4] The Spirit serves us as precursor of the
incarnate Word. He also reveals the Word. For Christ really
comes to our assemblies; he enters in and calls each of us in order
to draw all of us to the Father. It is as a result of the Lord's thus
coming as the Father's Word that the community of believers
becomes an assembly that will celebrate the Eucharist.[5]

When the Lord comes to us, he touches our heart and
summons it to turn around; he knocks on the door—will
we open it to him? This turning and openness are our first
conversion, which serves as a prelude to the conversion in
the anaphora when the entire offering will be changed into
him. "The doors were closed in the room where the disciples were", but "Jesus came and stood among them", and
"the disciples were filled with joy at seeing the Lord" (Jn
20:19–20). Jesus does not yet speak to us, but he is present.
The risen Christ cannot force open the doors of our hearts,
but as soon as we welcome him by the loving conversion
that faith effects, we experience the new joy of his presence:
conversion opens us to adoration.[6] Adoration and the turn-

[4] For example, by means of antiphons, an Introit, a litany, an exhortation.
[5] This is the point of the gospel procession: Christ in his person is the Gospel, the good news.
[6] By its nature, the "penitential liturgy" culminates in adoration (the tris-
agion of the Eastern liturgies, the *Gloria* of the Latin and Anglican liturgies).

ing of the heart are the ebb and flow of the Church's prayer when the Spirit reveals to her her Lord, who is coming. When the glory of the Father shines upon us from the face of Christ, the living wonder we feel only illumines more fully the night of absence in which sin had imprisoned us. Adoration without "metanoia" of heart would be hypocrisy, but a conversion that is not followed by an exodus, a going forth to the Father's love, would be a moralistic illusion and would end in despair. Conversion is theological, even doxological, and adoration is a reentry into the Father's will. If this movement is celebrated authentically and with faith, we begin to be transfigured; we are no longer onlookers at a theophany, but are ourselves enveloped in the cloud: the epiphany of Christ becomes ours and the Church's.

Then comes the event that is the Gospel. We first listen to the apostles, the witnesses to the Gospel, in the "reading" of the epistle. Then the risen Christ gives us his peace by giving us his Spirit (Jn 20:19–22). This is the moment of the epiclesis in the liturgy of the word, the synergy hidden in the "proclamation" of the Gospel. In the Holy Spirit the words of Jesus are more than a form of teaching; they become an event. "I say and thereby I accomplish": these words of the prophets are never truer than at this moment. The incarnate Word arises in the heart of the Church under the action of the Spirit. This is the only word the Father can understand: he gave it to us in the economy; it returns to him in the liturgy. It was sown in the only-begotten Son; now it bears fruit in the adopted children. Yes, the word leaps forth and moves toward communion with him; that is why there is a celebration, a "liturgy" of the word.

The Spirit reveals the Word to the Church. The word that is "given" then turns our humanity into the Bride of the Lamb. The more we listen to the Word made flesh and receive him, the more we become his body: "today" he whom we hear "is fulfilled" in us (see Lk 4:21). That is why the liturgy of the word requires a certain amount of time and a depth of silence; these together allow the word to be given and received. So distracted are we by noise when the Spirit gathers us that a simple "reading" of the texts, spiced up by a few monotonous verses, is insufficient. There must be a celebration, for the mystery is endeavoring to achieve its completion in us!

The Spirit is the living breath that is present in the word; he calls us, but will we respond? The Church, which we constitute here and now, is indeed "local", and we are called in order that we may be sent to "the scattered children of God" in this place. The epiphany in which the Lord transfigures us must not fade away when we leave the church. The point of the homily and the intercessions that follow it is to break the bread of the word for our hungry hearts so that we will share the mysterious hunger of the incarnate Word: "I have food to eat that you know not about" (Jn 4:32); "Let us go elsewhere, to the neighboring country towns, so that I can proclaim the message there too, because *that is why I came*" (Mk 1:38); "I have ardently longed to eat this Passover with you" (Lk 22:14).

The Eucharistic Anaphora

The second synergy of the Spirit and the Church has for its purpose to make the Passage of Jesus become ours. The liturgy of the word leads toward this memorial. Not, however, simply in order to revive the memory of it, as if the hour of Jesus were in the past; rather the anaphora brings a new time into existence. Not in order to repeat the hour of Jesus; rather it is we who become present to the crucified and risen Christ. No, the purpose is to accomplish in us, the members of his body, what he experienced once and for all.

By means of the faith that the Holy Spirit arouses in us at this moment, he no longer simply prepares our hearts for the Lord who is coming; rather he enables them to "enter the sanctuary, by a new way which he has opened for us, a living opening through the curtain, that is to say, his flesh" (Heb 10:19–20). Whatever may be the "sacramental units" preceding the great eucharistic prayer in the various liturgical traditions, in this prayer itself the Spirit brings us into the reality that is the body of Christ. He draws us into the depths of his living plan and into the abyss of death proper to the last times, where the risen Jesus comes looking for men: "having loved those who were his in the world, he loved them to the end", to the utmost of love (Jn 13:1). This is the point of the Creed, which draws the assembly together in faith in the Blessed Trinity and in its economy of salvation; it is the meaning also of the offerings and especially of the procession with the gifts, which resembles the entrance of Christ into the new Jerusalem; and the meaning of the kiss of peace, which is a sign of our communion in the love into which the Lord is drawing us.[7]

The event of Christ's Passage is thus what is celebrated in the eucharistic anaphora. In it the Gospel is fulfilled, as the Spirit "lifts up our hearts" to make us share in the Lord's Ascension, in the jubilant return to the Father in which the whole of reality, which is God's gracious gift, is at last delivered

---

[7] The place of the Creed, the presentation of the gifts, the procession with the gifts, and the kiss of peace vary from one liturgical family to another. On the meaning of the kiss of peace at this particular point in the Mass (before the anaphora) see Mt 5:23–24; Jn 13:1–15; Jn 20:19–20.

from death and becomes "thanksgiving".[8] The "eucharistic prayer" as a set of words is powerless to express this "great and marvelous" Passover of the Word and the Spirit, which like a seed was sown at the beginning of time and henceforth returns to him in the body of his beloved Son, each time bringing in an ever fuller measure its harvest of life. It is understandable, then, that the living tradition of the Churches should have created a multitude of eucharistic prayers and that Serapion, at the end of his own eucharistic prayer, should cry, "Let the Lord Jesus and his Holy Spirit speak in us and through our voices celebrate your ineffable mysteries!" The eternal liturgy that Isaiah glimpsed in the temple of the universe echoes in the song of the new Jerusalem: "Holy, holy, holy . . . heaven and earth are filled with his glory!" In the celebrated Eucharist the "prayer" and the mystery become one: everything is recapitulated in the body of Christ (Eph 1:10).

In the anamnesis that follows[9] we "remember" all the wonderful things the Blessed Trinity has done for mankind, and we gather them up in the "cup of synthesis",[10] in the center of love that is the body of the Lord Jesus in the hour of his Passage. In him God is wholly "given up" to men, and they are at last restored to God. "I shall be your God, and you shall be my people": the New Covenant is completed. The body of Christ embodies for us the sacrifice of love that is eternally being accomplished in the communion of the three Persons[11] and that now sanctifies for God's glory all that human sin had defiled. "This is my body that is given for

[8] "Ana-phora": the movement of carrying (*pherein*) on high (*ana* = up). "Eucharist": thanks-giving.
[9] "Anamnesis": remembering, making commemoration of.
[10] Saint Irenaeus.
[11] See chap. 1.

you. . . . This is my blood that is shed for the many." The body and the blood? Saint Irenaeus tells us: "It is then that death is overcome"; and Saint Ignatius of Antioch, "This is the medicine for immortality."

But who transforms our offerings into the body and blood of Christ if not the Spirit who acts in the Church? It is he who shows his power at the heart of this consecration; this is the key moment in the epiclesis. From the altar arises the cry of the crucified Word, mingled with the plea of the spouse: "Father, send your life-giving Spirit upon us and upon the gifts we offer. Turn this bread into the sacred Body of your Christ, and the contents of this cup into the precious Blood of your Christ, by transforming them through your Holy Spirit!" Jesus was raised from the dead once and for all because the Holy Spirit came to reward his radical self-giving to the Father's will; his death brought the gift of the Father's life. Here precisely is the poignant yet jubilant realism of the sacramental epiclesis. For the point of insertion of the liturgy into the last times is our death, the death that Jesus accepted in the utmost fullness of love. At this point the Father's compassion embraces the sufferings of all men and causes his Spirit to flow forth from the side of his beloved Son. It is this gift that comes to us in the epiclesis: the Spirit of Jesus permeates the death of men in order to give them his life. He pours himself out upon all flesh that offers itself to him, and his transforming energy gives the flesh a share in the Resurrection of Jesus; the wounded members are united to the incorruptible body and draw life from it.

The intercessions then bring the power of this eucharistic Pentecost to bear on everything that we offer to the Father. In union with Christ we stand before the face of the Father and intercede for all men: May the Holy Spirit come! He

who is "the place of the saints"[12] expands his presence
through our intercessions. The Church, in virginal faith, experiences with him the gestation of the world; supported solely
by the promise of him "who brings the dead to life" (Rom
4:17–20), she consents to be the new tomb wherein is laid
the human race that has been wounded by death. In its intercession, that is, in its epiclesis, the Church gives her freest
and most detached consent to the life-giving Spirit. In the
interceding Church human weakness becomes the living locus
in which the power of God acts; more astonishing still, the
sin of men becomes the crack through which healing and
the fullness of merciful grace come to them. The eucharistic
epiclesis, which exhibits its power in the intercessions, is the
moment of our lives in which our prayer is most "efficacious". Understandably, this intercession culminates in the
prayer of Jesus himself to our Father: in each petition the
Spirit is breathed forth and given.

The Eucharistic Communion

In the third movement of the eucharistic liturgy the Spirit
illumines "the eyes of our faith" by a vision of the Lamb of
God. Our sinful hearts recognize him and are bathed in his
light. Yes, the wedding feast of the Bride and the Lamb is
ready, and the Spirit draws us to it. See, the Lamb is raised
up, he gives us his peace, he is broken but not divided, and
he is at last about to give his life to those who will share in
the feast. This is the meaning of the little piece of eucharistic
bread that is mingled with the Blood in the cup, for he who
gave his body and shed his blood when he accepted our death

---

[12] Saint Basil of Caesarea.

is henceforth alive and gives us his life. A final epiclesis is celebrated at this point,[13] one that is correlative to the epiclesis in the liturgy of the word; in the mystery of the "two tables"[14] the faith that unites us to Christ comes to us from the Holy Spirit.

In the event of Communion the energy of the gift and the energy of its reception are fused into a single energy. We become the one whom we have received and in whom the Spirit has transformed us. The fruit of the Eucharist, to which all the power of the river of life is directed, is Communion, *koinōnia*, with the Blessed Trinity. The living out of the divine agape in the authenticity of our mortal flesh—that is the synergy of charity that will bear fruit in the liturgy of life. That is why this part of the liturgy is less developed in comparison with the two preceding parts.

In this banquet of the kingdom the gift is reciprocal and by its nature unreserved. In terms of the persons involved: I belong no longer to myself but to him who loved me and gave himself for me; he, in contrast, is now mine. If we have lived the liturgy of the word and the anaphora in all their spiritual realism, we will be transfigured and divinized, from new beginning to new beginning, in the light of Communion. This is the moment of the marriage of the Lamb who carries and takes away the sin of the world. Henceforth

[13] Hardly perceptible in the Western liturgies, this epiclesis is more developed in the East and especially in the Byzantine tradition in the symbol of the boiling water (*zeon*) that is poured into the chalice, to the accompaniment of these words: "The fervor of faith comes from the Holy Spirit." The celebrant has just said, while putting a fragment of the bread into the chalice, "The fullness of faith, the Holy Spirit", and, while blessing the boiling water, "Blessed be the fervor of your saints", i.e., of those who will be receiving Communion.

[14] The expression "two tables" is from Origen: the table of the word of Christ and the table of the body of Christ make up the single mystery of the bread of life (Jn 6).

my sin, my death, the despairing void of love in me, my impenetrable heart, the image which I am and which should radiate the splendor of his face: all these are no longer "mine"; the possessive "mine" is precisely what destroys the trinitarian Communion. No, we belong to him, and he belongs to the Father; we shall have life from him as he has life from the Father. The Communion thus completes the epiclesis of the anaphora in which the Spirit had entered into the depths of our hell in order to incorporate us into the incorruptible body.

"Adam, where are you?" The thirst of the living God as he sought humanity in the first paradise is quenched at the Communion. Adam, the fearful man, is found at last, and Jesus, the new Adam, makes him stand up and come forth into the perfect love that casts out fear. Having become one with us in our depths, the beloved Son now draws us to the Father: "Arise from among the dead! Arise, and let us go from here, for you are in me and I in you; together we form a single indivisible being. . . . Arise, and let us go from here, from death to life, from corruption to immortality, from darkness to everlasting light!"[15]

In Communion we anticipate the breakthrough of the Resurrection. From celebration to celebration the Church that is ourselves effects the passage of all creation. During the great Holy Saturday we were all in this Adam whom Christ wrests from death because he has reached the term of his Communion with men. Each time the divine liturgy is celebrated the Lord becomes "all" in us, in movement "toward his beginning that has no end",[16] and reaching at last the heart of the Blessed Trinity.

[15] Easter homily of Pseudo-Epiphanius.
[16] Saint Gregory of Nyssa.

From Prelude to Finale

The synergy of the Spirit and the Church that sustains the three movements of the celebration has a prelude and finale, which we often fail to appreciate. In a first blessing the Holy Spirit opened us to the liturgy about to be celebrated; in a final blessing he sends us forth to the liturgy of life. In the last analysis, the Eucharist runs its course between two kenoses: that of the Word in his personal body and that of the Spirit in the body of Christ that is the Church. Our celebration moves from the icon of the nativity to the icon of Pentecost. But since throughout the divine liturgy that Spirit has made us live within ourselves the event of Jesus' Passage, we must be attentive to the life he is going to live with us after the celebration. Having become the Church, we must live the Church's life as a kenosis of the Spirit. The gift to us of God's ever faithful love must be answered by an authentic life of the charity that the Holy Spirit pours into our hearts. We too must give our gift fully; that is, we must divest ourselves of ourselves in the same kenosis of love, so that we will belong solely to him. That is how the sacrifice is to be completed in us, that is, in the Church.

As the communion of God with humanity, the Church can only be hidden and transparent to the Spirit. What does the Church of the last times know of the children to whom she gives birth? She does know those whom she baptizes in water and the Spirit, but what of the others? Does she know all those who at each moment are born into the heavenly liturgy and whom the Father receives with eternal joy? Only when "the perfect Man", the total Christ with its full stature, appears in glory (Eph 4:13) will the Bride be able to lift up her eyes and say in her heart, "Who has borne me these? I was bereft and barren, exiled, turned out of my home; who has reared these? I was left all alone, so where have these come from?" (Is 49:18–21). Then they will say of the Church, "Everyone was born there" (Ps 87:5).

Chapter 12

The Sacramental Epicleses

For us who live in the last times the Eucharist is the supreme celebration of the liturgy. But if the mystery of Christ is manifested, made present, and communicated in this divine liturgy, why do the apostolic Churches celebrate other sacraments? They acknowledge as major sacraments baptism and chrismation, the reconciliation of penitents and the anointing of the sick, marriage and the ordained ministry. But why has the Lord given these signs of his Covenant to the Church, and why does his Spirit transfigure us by means of these other energies, when the whole body of Christ is given in the Eucharist? The sacrament of sacraments itself provides the answer.

During this time of gestation for the body of Christ the Church celebrates the Eucharist, and the Eucharist "accomplishes" the Church.[1] We "are able" to celebrate the Eucharist because communion with the Blessed Trinity has "already" been given to us, along with our new being, through baptism and the seal of the Spirit, but also because some members of the Church have been ordained for the service of the epiclesis that effects the Eucharist. However, we "ought" to celebrate the Eucharist because the divine communion is "not yet" complete in us and does not exist in everyone. The body of Christ has not yet acquired the strength it will

[1] In Christian usage, to "celebrate" is to accomplish the mystery.

have when it reaches full maturity (Eph 4:13). The experience of the other sacramental energies has its place in this movement of growth; the dynamism of ascension toward the definitive parousia finds expression in them.

But what is the special meaning of each of the synergies of Spirit and Church within the unity of the body? What is their connection with the sacrament of sacraments, since they are not six "others" to be set alongside it? It is useless to try to deduce the necessity of the major sacraments from the Eucharist or to search the letter of the New Testament for a juridical institution of each. In fact, the opposite seems to be the case: Christ and his Spirit gradually gave them to the Church on the basis of its life, to meet the structural and vital needs of the body as it grew. To discover the unity, diversity, and harmony of these energies, we must place ourselves once again at their source. Through them, the light of the transfiguration divinizes men at the points at which they look to be saved; when everything has turned into light, the sacraments will disappear, and the body of Christ will be real forever.

Unity and Diversity of the Sacramental Energies

The fontal liturgy exists prior to the sacramental celebrations; it gives them life and enables them to bear their fruit. The mystery is not divided up between six sacraments; rather the one body of the Lord radiates the pure light of its Wisdom[2] in distinct energies; when these energies are united

[2] See Wis 7:22–8:1. Wisdom was the name most widely used for the Spirit in the first three centuries, just as Logos (Word) was the name most widely used for the Son.

to those of the Church to which they give rise, the result is the sacramental synergies. In each of these the economy of salvation is celebrated. It is true, of course, that in the least movement of a believing heart that responds, however poorly, to the love of its Lord, the Holy Spirit, and the disciple of Jesus are in synergy, but the entire economy of salvation is not accomplished in such moments. This, however, is what does happen in the sacraments. In each of them we experience the three movements of the Passage of Jesus: the Father gives us his beloved Son, the Word assumes our flesh and our death in order to raise us up with himself, and his Spirit brings us into the eternal communion of the Father.

However, a celebration is a synergy of the Spirit and the Church as Church. In the river of life the Spirit and the Bride are united in a single kenosis, to the point where from their two wills flows a single love. In the anointing of a sick person or the ordination of a deacon—to take examples of celebrations that seem limited to a single individual—the Spirit and the Church act in a member of the Lord's body, but they do so for the sake of the life of the entire body. A sacramental synergy is distinguished from the many indescribable synergies that fill the lives of the saints by the fact that in the sacraments the Church as such activates her energy of receptivity and faith. She cooperates, as the Church, with the life-giving energy of the Paraclete.

Finally, in every sacrament, however unobtrusive, all the actors in the eternal liturgy are at work. The Blessed Trinity pours out its divinizing energies and is glorified. The communion of the angels and saints takes part in the saving of its members who are still in the great tribulation, and it celebrates this salvation with unceasing praise. And what shall we say of the comprehensive love that is the divine agape:

the communion of Churches that are still pilgrims in this world? Some poor man or woman rediscovers the Father's mercy; a couple wagers their future in marriage; an unknown sick person experiences a rebirth of hope from the oil poured out by the Spirit's tender love: all these hidden wonders the Church accomplishes in the communion of Churches. Then all the members suffer and all are raised up, for we are all members of one another.

But this communion does not fuse us into an anonymous collectivity that follows a uniform rhythm. On the contrary, the unity of the body is manifested in the organic diversity of its synergies. The Spirit and the Church act in various sacraments because the members are many and have many needs for eternal life and many functions in the body of Christ. The inexhaustible source of this diversity is the Father's love for mankind and for each individual without reserve. Each person is unique because he is acknowledged and loved in the one body of the beloved Son. Whereas in the Eucharist this love "is accomplished" for the entire body, in the other sacraments it is given to individuals according to their needs, their age, their gifts in Christ. In the unique sacrament that is the body of Christ each sacramental synergy communicates a gift of the Holy Spirit. This is why each sacrament is distinguished from the others by its special epiclesis. At this point in the celebration the Church is simply a "handmaid of the Lord". She asks the Father that the Spirit of Jesus may be poured out on the member of his body that is here being offered. In this context the divinizing energy of the Paraclete is a response of tender love and fidelity, of grace and truth. And if we are attentive to the epiclesis of each sacrament, we will see that the sacramental energies correspond in a vital way to the three moments in the growth of the body of Christ.

The Epicleses of Birth

In baptism and chrismation the foundational energy of the Spirit is poured out in the members of the Church. As sacraments of the beginning of our new existence in Christ, they are celebrated only once. Only once are we born and given an organic structure in the Holy Spirit. The first gift that the Church seeks to offer to the Father is her children, all the scattered children of God who are born according to the flesh but are still in death. She is the spouse, and the first movement that makes itself felt in her due to the attraction of the Spirit is the passionate desire of the Father; in the economy of his love everything proceeds from this desire: God's glory is man fully alive![3] This desire of the Father becomes the Church's own desire in the epiclesis of baptism. The first plea of the Virgin Church finds expression in her faith-inspired gift of herself: let your Son come! Through me and by the power of your Spirit let children be born to you in your beloved Son! The epiclesis of baptism is for birth according to the Spirit.

It is true, of course, that that which is offered is already "in the image" of its God, but the icon is disfigured and broken; it "lacks God's glory" (Rom 3:23); it has not yet been born to the life of its Father. Its parents have given it everything: existence, biological and psychic heredity, education and culture. They have still to offer it what they cannot themselves give it: freedom, the power to become free of all these determinisms, a divine creativity, or, in short, true incorruptible life, the life of the living God. This is the only gift they cannot give their child, but it is the gift that will enable all the others to bear fruit beyond death. When the

[3] Saint Irenaeus.

parents take this step, they share in the faith of the Church; they are caught up in the movement of self-donation; they look for everything from the power of the Holy Spirit. They contribute their energy of receptivity and response to the epiclesis that will be celebrated.

When catechumens are immersed in the waters of baptism, that is, in the name of the Father, of the Son, and of the Holy Spirit, they are really "baptized" because they participate in what the epiclesis has made real beforehand. The actual moment of baptism is analogous to the moment of Communion at the Eucharist. But the epiclesis that makes baptism possible has consisted in the coming of the Holy Spirit into the water in which the catechumens are to be baptized. The faithful, and perhaps even celebrants, are too often unconscious of the consecration of the baptismal water. Water is the symbol of primordial life. In the maternal womb it has already become more than a symbol. But it is in birth into the life of the Blessed Trinity that the symbol turns into full reality. Every epiclesis is a sacramental Pentecost, but here the Spirit really descends,[4] enters into the water, and transforms it into a "divine milieu". This new reality is the maternal womb of the Church, in which a man who is born of flesh and blood and human desire will be immersed in order that it may be born of the Spirit and the Bride. The virginal fruitfulness of the Church is the masterpiece of the Spirit. This is how the sons of God are born (Jn 1:12–13).

This astounding epiclesis shows that the Holy Spirit gives life to men by bringing them into communion in the body of Christ. We had occasion to wonder earlier at this marvelous phenomenon when we contemplated the coming of the

---

[4] The water is not altered chemically any more than the bread and wine are by the eucharistic epiclesis. The reality is nonetheless new.

Church on the first Pentecost.[5] Here the wonder is even more striking. We do not first become children of God, members of Christ, temples of the Holy Spirit, and then children of the Church; no, the Church comes first.[6] The Church is this primordial water that is permeated by the divinizing energy of the Spirit, and it is the Church that gives birth. In the last times does not the Church bear Christ in the mysterious gestation in which she offers the world to the "life-giving" Spirit? In the celebration of a baptism the Church bears a child of the Father; it is through the Church that the day of the Resurrection dawns, which knows no setting. It is through the Church's faith, combined with the power of the Spirit, that a catechumen is "grafted" into Christ and incorporated into the incorruptible body. The Church then gives the Father a new adopted child, who is configured to the beloved Son. That is how this man becomes "new" and lives with the life of the Blessed Trinity. All the other "effects" of baptism flow from this epiclesis.[7]

It is possible that misunderstanding of the epiclesis in baptism is one reason for the practical depreciation of confirmation in some Churches. Chrismation, the second sacrament of Christian initiation, is in danger of passing unnoticed if we make no distinctions and see baptism as simply birth into divine life. The question that then arises is the one suggested by the common sense of parents who are in any degree aware of what is going on: If our child has become a child of God through baptism, why should he be confirmed? If baptism gives the child a share in the life of the Father, the Son, and the Holy Spirit, why does he have to receive the Holy Spirit

[5] See chap. 5.

[6] The Church began to baptize on Pentecost; therefore the children of God are born of water and the Spirit.

[7] See Saint John Chrysostom, *Third Baptismal Instruction*, no. 5.

in "confirmation"? Did he not receive the Spirit in baptism? And yet the practice of the early Church, beginning in the Acts of the Apostles,[8] and the unbroken tradition of the Eastern Churches are clear on the subject: baptism and the personal gift of the Spirit are distinct but inseparable, with the second completing the first. Christians are baptized in a single Spirit in order to form a single body, *and* they are given the same Spirit to drink.[9]

Throughout the development of his plan for human redemption and divinization, the Father constantly sends his Son and his Spirit. In this mission Son and Spirit are linked, but they remain distinct. In the fullness of time it is the Son who is incarnated, but it is the Spirit who incarnates him. On the first Pentecost, which marks the beginning of the last times, the Church is formed as the body of Christ, but it is the Spirit that does the forming. From that moment on, the Spirit causes the body to grow by joining new members to her, and this birth takes place in baptism. But in that moment of birth the Lord pours out his own fullness on these members, that is, he gives them his Spirit in a very personal way; this personal gift of the Spirit to the person of the neophyte is the sacramental synergy of confirmation.

This manifestation and outpouring of the Spirit are at the heart of what we are looking for throughout the present book. For this is the point of origin in which the wellspring of worship becomes the life of the Christian as a new being. If we stop at baptism as a participation in the divine life, we risk living our lives under the sign of a unipersonal monotheism; we have not as yet reached the communion of the three Persons. It is the Holy Spirit who brings us across the

[8] Acts 2:38; 8:15–17; 10:44–48; 19:5–9.
[9] 1 Cor 12:13.

threshold from the one to the other. If we fail to cross it, we can construct systems of Christian humanism, but we will be blind to "theology", to the "mystical" life. The baptized are organically structured only because the same Spirit who "anointed" Christ penetrates the members of Christ in their entirety as body, soul, and spirit. Only then do these members become "Christians", that is, anointed with the Spirit. Then a new vital principle dynamizes them and gradually expands and deepens their communion with the Father and the Son.

The epiclesis of confirmation, which is spoken when the bishop consecrates the holy chrism[10] that will anoint the members of the baptized, has for its specific content the marvelous total gift Christ the Lord makes of himself in this anointing: he hands over his own personal Spirit and engraves or imprints this Spirit on the hearts of those to whom he has just been united forever. "The seal of the gift of the Holy Spirit"[11] gives the baptized a participation in the synergy of the fontal liturgy; the Spirit is henceforth united with the spirits of the baptized so that the latter may live a wholly new life in which the two wills can produce the one fruit of the Spirit.[12] The Spirit has become the life of the baptized and therefore guides their conduct (Gal 5:25). The mystery of the Spirit and the Bride will no longer be contemplated simply as a gift awaited and desired; rather, those who have just been raised to life with Jesus will really participate in

---

[10] See Saint Cyril of Jerusalem, *Third Mystagogical Catechesis*, no. 3: "Do not think that this is ordinary oil. Just as after the epiclesis of the Holy Spirit the bread of the Eucharist is no longer simply bread but the Body of Christ, so this holy oil is no longer ordinary, not to say common oil, but a gift of Christ and the presence of the Holy Spirit; it is filled with the energy of his divinity."

[11] Byzantine Euchologion.

[12] Rom 8:16; Gal 5:22–23.

that mystery. In the fullness given with the Holy Spirit, all the gifts and charisms needed for the neophyte's growth are already contained. And the very first of these gifts is the priestly energy that enables the confirmed henceforth to celebrate the divine liturgy[13] and cooperate with the sacramental energies that sustain them on their exodus to the kingdom.

The Epicleses of Healing, or the Victory over Death

The one whom the Lord places as a seal on our hearts is faithful; he is strong, and not simply as strong as death but stronger than death; he is the flame of the love of our God (see Song 8:6). For a harsh struggle, lasting as long as the crossing of the wilderness, awaits those who have just put on the armor of God (Eph 6:11).

The first key struggle is the confrontation with the power of death that still smoulders in the baptized, even though it has been virtually conquered in the passage of baptism. We are "already" holy, but we are "not yet" fully configured to the Lord. The anointing with his Spirit must slowly penetrate all the fibers of our being, rectify our rebellious wills, purify our motives, set our innate urges free, and integrate everything with our hearts wherein his love is meant to reign. In this work of bringing the new man in us to its full stature, the Spirit of Jesus always begins by revealing our sinfulness to us. Apart from the Spirit we may feel guilty; only in him do we recognize ourselves to be sinners. And the more he

---

[13] The Eucharist completes Christian initiation. The Orthodox Churches have kept the primitive tradition of joining the three sacraments in a single celebration.

transforms our hearts by uniting them to the Father's will, the more we discover how poor in love of the Father we are. The stream of mercy and the abyss of wretchedness meet in an agonizing synergy: the synergy of forgiveness. When the synergy becomes sacramental, it shows itself either as conversion (if the emphasis is put on the turning of the heart that the Holy Spirit brings about) or as reconciliation (if it is seen primarily as the recovery of communion in Christ with the Father and with our brothers). But conversion and reconciliation are inseparable, just as are the two aspects of sin that they heal: rejection and rupture. The wound suffered by sinners, along with the wounds in their brothers, has been endured by Jesus in his death, and it is from this crucified love that the Spirit who gives communion streams forth. For he is in his person "the forgiveness of our sins": where the relationship with the Father has been lacking[14] or has even been broken, the Spirit, who is "the Father's tender love",[15] pours himself out and becomes the living bond of love that unites persons. He is the blood of communion that causes the members of the body to draw life from the life of the Father.

The epiclesis proper to this sacrament—and how inattentive we are to it!—consists in this outpouring of the Holy Spirit. It is his kenosis of love in the hearts of sinners who consent to open themselves to the Father's compassion. In the key moment of the "absolution" everything is "loosed" because everything is set free by the communion that is the Spirit of the Lord. The priest's prayer is a true epicletic prayer.[16] The priest, who is a living sign of Christ the Servant,

---

[14] To "sin" (Hebrew, *hata'a*) means to "miss the mark".

[15] This beautiful name for the Holy Spirit is an allusion to the biblical word *hesed*.

[16] The Latin form of absolution, which is more declarative and juridical, must not be allowed to blur our sense of the epiclesis.

intercedes that this son of the Father, "who was dead", may "come back to life"; the entire intercession of the praying Church is gathered up in the priest as he prays that this person for whom Christ died may rise to new life. This gift corresponds to the answer of the returning prodigal: mercy is offered to the prodigal on the sole condition that he wills to return to the Father and to the brethren with the same love.

It is true, of course, that on the altar of our hearts we can ceaselessly offer the bread of tears for our sins and that the fire of the Spirit can inflame us ever anew. But who can deny that there are moments in our lives when our accumulated rejections and ruptures are such that we cannot honestly avoid confessing our sins and being reconciled to the community? "Insofar as you did this to one of the least of these brothers of mine, you did it to me": this statement holds for giving them death as well as giving them life. In the epiclesis of this sacrament "the unity of the Spirit" among the members is reestablished "by the peace that binds you together" (Eph 4:3). This is the mystical sense, which goes beyond the simple moral will, of reconciliation with Christ. Every sin, even the most secret, has inflicted a wound on the body; the member must therefore be healed in the body. If we thus pay close attention to the Spirit in this epiclesis, we shall, through the healing of our sin, recapture the freshness proper to the Church; we shall rediscover the true face of the Lord, no longer obscured by the idols that our moral conscience and frustrated superego erect; above all, we shall enter into the joy of the Father, as our return gladdens his angels and the communion of saints.[17]

---

[17] See Lk 15 and the thrust of the Confiteor, in which the rejoicing of God's entire family is the setting for reconciliation.

"Holy Father, physician of our souls and our bodies";[18] these are the words that begin the epiclesis of the other sacrament—the anointing of the sick—by which our chronic sickness is cured. Forgiveness, that is, the outpouring of the Spirit who establishes communion, attacks death at its root and its most hidden sting, namely, sin (1 Cor 15:56). The anointing of the Spirit, this mysterious oil that penetrates our mortal bodies, is like the new myrrh that the Spouse pours on the suffering members of her Lord. "Myrrh is for the dead; the body of Christ remains incorruptible."[19] The evident wounds of sin that little by little furrow our bodies are thus healed in hope.

The epiclesis of this sacrament anticipates for each of us our complete resurrection, and this is again the work of the Holy Spirit: "If the Spirit of him who raised Jesus from the dead has made his home in you, then he who raised Christ Jesus from the dead will give life to your own mortal bodies through his Spirit living in you" (Rom 8:11). In the synergy of our conversion, the baptism of water became a baptism of tears and of resurrection for the heart; in the anointing of the sick, the Spirit configures us to Jesus in his sufferings, transforms our weakness into life-giving love, and completes in our members the irresistible passage of him who is head of the body. Then that which Ezekiel glimpsed in his vision of the dry bones (Ezek 37:1–14) becomes a reality for us; the Spirit of life lays hold of us in our weakness, and the "seal of his gift" becomes a pledge of resurrection that nothing can take from us. Jesus healed the sick during his time on earth, thus restoring them to a life that must end. But when his

[18] Byzantine Euchologion.
[19] Troparion in the Office of the Compassion, which is celebrated on Good Friday evening in the Byzantine liturgy.

Spirit permeates our bodies that have been wounded by death, he causes them to pass beyond death: "Death is no more, because Christ our God is risen!" [20]

These two sacraments meet a constant need of the body of Christ during the last times: the need of overcoming death in its root, which is sin. The gradual divinization of the children of God can come to pass only through the gradual elimination of the movement of rebellion by which our wounded hearts are wrung. As sacraments of healing, they give the members of Christ a participation in the saving love of their Lord, who here and now takes upon himself their wounds of nature and of will. The frequency of these sacraments is not determined; it depends on the course of the divine health—sanctification—which Christians freely accept by joining their wills to the energy of the Holy Spirit.

The Epicleses of Christ the Servant: The Gift of Life

Marriage and the ordained ministry are the two sacramental synergies of adult life in Christ. They lay hold of persons in order to open them to the divinest of all the activities made available to men: the giving of the very life of God. Both synergies are at one and the same time charisms, that is, gifts of the Spirit for the good of all, and energies that divinize those who receive the charisms. Christians can give the life of God only by giving their own lives, as the Lord did, but this gift of self will be the more fruitful in the degree that these persons have themselves been transformed into him whom they are giving. These are not transitory charisms geared to limited purposes but functional and structural syn-

---

[20] Troparion of the Resurrection, sixth mode, in the Byzantine liturgy.

ergies or, to put it more accurately, organic charisms by which "the whole body is fitted and joined together" (Eph 3:11–16).

The novelty of sacramental marriage is to be found in the epiclesis, in which the betrothed receive the gift of the Holy Spirit. We need a sharp reminder of this, because there is widespread the naive view that marriage is simply a contract in which the spouses are the ministers.[21] Their consents are indeed necessary as being the energy at work in the human response, but they must not be allowed to make us forget the energy of the divine gift. It is noteworthy that the famous passage of Paul on the subject of marriage (Eph 5:32) speaks precisely of the mystery that transforms the union of husband and wife, and not the other way around. What the sacrament adds is not so much the blessing of the couple (every marriage, after all, is holy) as the love of Christ and his Church in which the husband and wife will share. The mystery comes first; it both reveals the divine meaning of the union of the spouses and makes that meaning a reality in them.

In most cultures the state of marriage is symbolized by the idea of "covenant". In a sacramental marriage there is a personal covenant uniting bridegroom and bride, but "bridegroom and bride" here refer inseparably to Christ and the Church and to this man and this woman. The covenant, however, is the Holy Spirit himself. He is the source of the unity of this undivided love; he is its divine bond, which human sin cannot break. He is the communion that establishes a new relationship within the family, the "domestic Church". In this "house of God" the mystery of the Church as communion is always "visible". The new element in a specifically sacramental marriage transforms the spouses

---

[21] If this were indeed the case, it is difficult to see why the couple could not abrogate their contract by common consent.

first of all; beyond all opposition between the spouses and all thought of superiority on the one or other side, the relationship of the two can be constantly renewed so as to share in the transparency of the union of Christ and the Church. The new element also transforms their mutual gift of life to their children and, in addition, gives this gift of life an unpredictable fruitfulness that extends to all their forms of creativity and service.[22]

The ordained ministry is to the forefront of the mystery of service in the body of Christ. Its epiclesis, which is signified by the laying on of hands,[23] is entirely original in that it pours out upon some members the most hidden and most selfless ecclesial energy, for it makes them servants of the other sacramental epicleses. This "ordination" is one of the most astonishing proofs of the Lord's fidelity; it means that despite the failings of his envoys, he will never deprive his Church of the gifts of his Spirit. "Whether Peter or Judas do the baptizing, it is Christ who baptizes."[24] The Spirit will always act with power in the sacraments, through the "vessels of clay", that is, the ordained ministers of Christ.

Whatever the degrees[25] or contingent forms of these services, the new element in them cannot be reduced to a

---

[22] The charism of religious life complements that of marriage in the Church (see 1 Cor 7), but it is not a sacrament; the gift of virginity, which is the basis of religious life, "already" gives a participation in the world of the Resurrection (Lk 21:35–36).

[23] The laying on of hands is a biblical symbol for the transmission of the power of the Holy Spirit.

[24] Saint Augustine.

[25] The bishop and the presbyteral college, which extends to a plurality the one charism of the bishop, are ordained to the "priesthood"; there is an imposition of hands on deacons, "not for priesthood but for ministry" (formula taken from the Egyptian Church Order and adopted by Vatican II in its Constitution on the Church, no. 29).

social function of guidance or administration; rather, it has its roots deep in the mystery of the kenosis of Christ. At this level nothing makes sense except in relation to love, and I mean not only the love poured out in the hearts of bishop, priest, or deacon, but also and above all the love that is the very energy at work in their service. In their service the Spirit flows in abundance from the side of the crucified Lord, because in these weak men it is Christ himself who is servant of his Church, to the point of being everything in it. The mystery of kenosis here is the kenosis of the shepherd who gives his life for his flock. Whereas in marriage man and woman share in the love that unites Christ and the Church into a single body, here the servants manifest Christ as distinct from his Bride, Christ as servant of his Church. He calls the Church, gives her his word, reveals the Father to her, enlightens her, forgives her, feeds her with his body and blood, strengthens and sends her, purifies and transfigures her, makes her fruitful, and causes her to bring the world to birth in the kingdom, and this with all the energies of his love. Here the Holy Spirit is the liturgy, and his ministers are its servants. These ministers do not repeat or make otiose the prophetic, priestly, and kingly functions of the other members of the Church; on the contrary, they are with and for these other members; they are their servants. It is to this function, which is structural and not provisional, of service to the Church that their entire ministry is "ordained".

The Sacramental Harmony of the Body of Christ

Once we have properly situated the major sacraments as synergies within the body of Christ, we can perhaps understand better their harmony with the sacrament of sacraments, the Eucharist.

If the central event in the Eucharist is the epiclesis that wholly transforms the body of Christ, then the epicleses that are constitutive of the other sacraments must evidently be organically related to the epiclesis of the Eucharist. In the Eucharist the sacramental Pentecost embraces the entire body; in the other sacraments it touches the members according to their ages, their needs, and their gifts in Christ. In baptism the Holy Spirit bestows birth into communion with the Trinity within the body; in chrismation he makes this participation personal by himself becoming the indefectible energy of the new member. In the reconciliation of sinners and the anointing of the sick he exercises his power to give life from Resurrection to Resurrection. In marriage and the ordained ministry, he, "the Lord who gives life", enables the Spouse to share her fruitful virginity; more accurately, he communicates to the members of the Church, each according to his gift, the "nothing is impossible to God" that he has already made a reality in the Church.

If the river of life streams out in the Eucharist as integral liturgy and all-powerful synergy, the major sacraments are, as it were, the channels that bring water to the new Jerusalem. The sacramental synergies flow from the Eucharist and lead back to it.

They flow from the Eucharist as the light radiates from the transfigured body of the Lord. So true is this that the Church celebrates the major sacraments in the same way that she celebrates the sacrament of the body of Christ: under a eucharistic form. Despite all the diversity in the liturgical families, our Churches celebrate each sacrament after the manner of the divine liturgy. From baptism to ordained ministry we find in each the three stages that mark the Eucharist, the three synergies of the Spirit and the Church: a liturgy of the word; an anaphora with its high point, the epiclesis; and a liturgy of communion. In each sacrament the Spirit manifests, makes really present, and communicates the life of the body of Christ. That which distinguishes each sacrament from the others is the energy of the Holy Spirit that is asked for in the epiclesis.

The sacramental synergies also lead back to the Eucharist, for it is the Eucharist that "makes" or "accomplishes" the Church. In each the body is built up and grows organically by the power of the Spirit and the response of the members to whom the power of the Spirit is given. In the final analysis, this harmony is the harmony of the *koinōnia*, that is, of the communion of the Blessed Trinity that permeates and raises up our humanity. In baptism and chrismation this communion is given as a new power of the living God that makes men alive. In the reconciliation of penitents and the anointing of the sick, the communion is renewed; the living icon is transfigured in its depths. In marriage and the ordained ministry communion is not only received but is given in order to be communicated to others. It is in this way that the Lord comes, that his reign becomes a reality, that his plenitude in all its fullness is poured out irresistibly on all. All this makes clear the profoundly "communal" significance of every sacramental celebration. The community that is present is, of course, involved in the celebration, but so is the communion of all the churches and the vastly greater communion, now in gestation, that encloses in the womb of the Church all men and the cosmos and history.

Thus the mystery, the "many-sided . . . wisdom" of God, is brought to fulfillment "through the Church" (Eph 3:10).

The communion of the Blessed Trinity that pervades us is here in a eucharistic state; that is, it takes the form of "thanksgiving" to him "whose power, working in us, can do infinitely more than we can ask or imagine; glory be to him from generation to generation in the Church and in Christ Jesus for ever and ever" (Eph 3:20–21).

Chapter 13

The Celebration of a New Time

We have seen that celebrations are "moments" in which the economy of salvation turns into liturgy in the last times. But the life-giving stream of the river of life does not flow only intermittently. Until his Ascension reaches its completion in the parousia, Christ constantly enfolds this world in the tender love of his Spirit. Jesus is risen and is the Lord of the history in which we are involved. He is, and he is coming. His irresistible coming includes more than the "moments" of our celebrations. In fact, these "moments" are possible only because they are the irruption into our mortal time of a living time that has been delivered from death. In other words, at the source of our celebrations is an energy of the Holy Spirit from which we must constantly drink, and this energy is the new time inaugurated by the Resurrection. It is this time that enters into our days, weeks, and years, until our old time is saturated with it, and the mortal veil that covers our old time is at last rent. But even now, "today", we can participate in this new time.

A Long, Everlasting Day of Light

This "today" of the living God, into which man can enter, is the hour of Jesus. His "passage" is the event that runs through all of history and sustains it.

See the sacred rays of the light of the glorious Christ. . . .
The vast, impenetrable night has been swallowed up and the
gloomy darkness destroyed by this light, and the dismal shadow
of death has retreated into the darkness. Life has reached out
to all and all have been filled with an intense light. The
supreme Orient invades the universe, and the great Christ
who existed, immortal and immense, "before the morning
star" and before the heavenly bodies, shines more brightly
than the sun upon all that exists. That is why a long, everlasting day of light that shall not be extinguished, the mystical Pasch, is dawning on us who believe in him.[1]

When we celebrate Christ our Passover, our time is permeated by this day; it is transfigured and becomes sacramental.
For this day does not arise out of the first creation, like the
days of which it is said, "Evening came and morning came."[2]
This is the day that is hymned in the Easter psalm: "This is
the day which Yahweh has made, a day for us to rejoice and
be glad."[3] It is not a day among others or like the others that
derive their rhythm from the rising and setting of the sun. It
is the light of life, which not even the twilight of death can
any longer dim; it is truly the fullness, the completion of
time.

But the radiant light of the day of the Resurrection does
not reach us simply in the form of a memory or an abstract
ideal, for if that were true, death would still have a hold upon
it. No, the form it takes is the unceasing energy of the Spirit
at work in our mortal time. It is not outside but within those
who receive it: "Our God is not above, but ahead of us in

[1] From a homily inspired by the treatise of Saint Hippolytus on the Pasch,
ed. P. Nautin (*Sources chrétiennes* 27), 116.
[2] Gen 1, passim.
[3] Ps 117(118):24.

the encounter which we await." [4] The encounter of the day of the Resurrection with our unrenewed time, of the new time offered by the Spirit and the time of the believer's experience: *that* is what turns our time into a sacramental time. How, then, does this sacramental time make its presence felt in the body of Christ as a result of the paschal celebration?

"A Year of Favor from the Lord" (Lk 4:19)

Starting on Easter as from its light-filled center, the new time of the Resurrection first sweeps through *the year.* We usually think of the year as the longest unit of experiential time, a unit determined by the cyclical course of our planet around its source of light. But when the light of incorruptible life streams from the tomb, it takes our cyclical year with it beyond the circle of death; repetition was an admission of impotence at the threshold of fullness. In addition, for those who are already risen with Christ, the year is drawn into the synergy of the eternal liturgy: it becomes "liturgical", if we understand "liturgical year" here not as a calendar of feasts but as the movement of the mystery in adapting itself to the rhythms of our experiential time. Starting from Easter and moving out to both sides of this center, the year is progressively transfigured by the liturgy and becomes sacramental. Each moment of its onward movement becomes a transparent sign of the day of the Resurrection and a prism for the liturgy in its plenitude.

Easter day is first of all the completion of a great week, which thereby also becomes sacramental: *Holy Week.* During the seven days that precede the celebration of the

---

[4] Saint Isaac of Nineveh.

Resurrection, the liturgical poem that is the week of the first creation is not nullified but fulfilled as it becomes a new creation in Christ. In order that everything might be fulfilled, in accordance with the final words of the Word in his mortal state (Jn 19:30), everything had to be assumed: from the first word of the Father, out of which streamed presence and life, to the final silence of absence and death into which men had sunk. In this eschatological light of fulfillment, we can rediscover the main stages of this week: the entrance of the Light into the world and among his own, and his rejection by our darkness;[5] the primordial testing of the freedom of men in regard to their essential food;[6] the Tree of Life, inaccessible to men who try to deify themselves, but offered to us in the incarnate Word, who divinizes us.[7] This great drama that is the economy of salvation reaches its climax on the sixth day, the great Friday on which the divine kenosis becomes our theophany: "Ecce homo—Behold the man!" (Jn 19:5). Then comes the great sabbath: the sabbath of God and his creation, the silence of the depths in which the Living One penetrates to the sources of all existence. In this descent of the incorruptible body into the lower world, the lie that is death melts away, the peace of the divine communion is spread abroad, hope becomes the beginning of everything, and the river of life carries everything along toward the consummation of time.

---

[5] Compare Gen 1:3, which speaks of the first kenosis of the light into creation, with the entrance of Jesus into Jerusalem in the lowliness of his flesh.

[6] Compare Gen 3, in which man snatches the fruit of the Tree of Life instead of receiving it as an unmerited gift, with what is said at the first Eucharist: "Take, eat, this is my Body which is given for you."

[7] Christ crucified is the true Tree of Life by which man is divinized.

For this reason, the week that follows upon the day of the Resurrection is no longer a week of chronological time but the extension and display of the day that has no evening. During the *week of renewal* the Easter liturgy is celebrated over and over, not as something being repeated but as something constantly new. This properly sacramental week becomes the prototype and even the matrix of all the weeks of the "liturgical" year. Sunday, the first day of the week, sheds the life-giving light of the Resurrection on all the other days. Saint Gregory of Nyssa tells us that "throughout the week that is their life" Christians "live out the one Pasch by making this time a time of light",[8] and Origen says, "There is not a moment when he [the Christian] is not keeping the Passover."[9]

If we take our stand at this center of light, we readily perceive the harmony of the "year of favor" during which the Lord communicates the fullness of his mystery to the Church. Before Holy Week and preparing the way for it are the seven weeks of *Lent*, during which we live out the stages of return to the paradise of the new creation. After Easter, and unfolding for us the newness of the Resurrection, are the seven weeks leading to *Pentecost*, the "fiftieth day", weeks during which the neophytes—all of us—learn to live in communion with our risen Lord. Finally, stretching out on either side of this paschal center are the two great seasons of the economy of salvation that has turned into liturgy: in the season of the *theophany*, or manifestation of the Son, the Word incarnate assumes our wretched body, and in the season of the *theosis*, or divinization by the Spirit, the Breath of the Lord configures us to his glorious body.

[8] PG 46:628CD.

[9] Origen, *Contra Celsum* 8:22, from *Origen: Contra Celsum*, trans. H. Chadwick (Cambridge, 1953), 468.

For it is always the body of Christ that grows through this celebration of sacramental time. The three great synergies of the Eucharist extend into the celebration of the liturgical year. To the liturgy of the word corresponds the season of *the manifestation of the Lord*, the season of Epiphany, which has for its focal point the decisive event of the baptism of Jesus. But the Church very quickly realized the importance of having a season of preparation (the Advent of the Western liturgies) that would be at once the beginning and the end of the sacramental year, the alpha and omega of the mystery, a memorial of the preparation for the Lord's first coming and a time of waiting for his Second Coming.

To the eucharistic anaphora corresponds the season of *the Passage of the Lord*, which is prepared for by Lent and culminates in the Ascension. Finally, to the liturgy of communion corresponds the time of *the outpouring of the Spirit*,[10] the time par excellence of the growing Church, of the apostles, of the transfiguration of Christ's body and its participation in his life-giving Cross. It is in the light of this communion that we grasp the meaning of the *sanctoral* as a celebration of the holy body of Christ: first of the holy Mother of God, the spotless one, the Virgin Mary, and then of all the other saints, whose communion is rightly celebrated as the fulfillment of Pentecost.[11] Then indeed does the river of life make the trees of life fruitful, "twelve times . . . once a month", that is, constantly. Thus the harvest of the Spirit anticipates even now the consummation of time.

---

[10] The name "time after Pentecost" is chronologically accurate but hardly suggests the mystery being celebrated during these months.

[11] The communion of "all the saints" is celebrated either at the end of the "time after Pentecost" (in the West) or on the octave day of the feast of Pentecost (in the East).

"The First Day of the Week"

The day of the Resurrection, which sheds its light upon the entire year and transfigures it, also penetrates the smallest units of our time. That is what we, together with Jesus, ask of his Father and ours: "Give us this day our necessary bread",[12] the bread of "this day". The sacramental day that transforms each moment of our lives into new time is *Sunday*, the "Lord's Day" (Rev 1:10). Because of the Eucharist, Sunday is indeed the efficacious memorial, the fruitful anamnesis that makes us present to the eternal liturgy and participants in it. It is the day of the assembly in which we really receive a foretaste of the communion of all the saints in the Blessed Trinity. It is the day on which through us our world mysteriously enters into the freedom of the sons of God for which it groans and which it anxiously awaits. Far from being a "holiday", it is the day on which "the Father still goes on working" (Jn 5:17) and grants us to share intensely in his creative and saving love. It is a day of rest indeed, but of the Rest of God in which the energy expended does not lead to the exhaustion of death but is an outpouring of life, joy, festivity, and creative liturgy.

"The perfect man, who is always engaged in the words, works, and thoughts of the divine Logos . . . is always living in his days and is continually observing the Lord's Day."[13] This energy of risen men, this "one thing necessary", is ours to live by at every moment. That is the miracle of which I shall be speaking when I turn to the liturgy as life.

---

[12] Greek: *epiousios;* Latin (Vulgate): *supersubstantialis.* The temporal meaning, "of this day *or* daily", that is usually given to *epiousios* is close to the qualitative sense ("necessary, essential") of the etymology followed in the liturgical mystery.

[13] Origen, *Contra Celsum* 8:22 (Chadwick, ibid.).

Meanwhile, however, there is one final sign that reveals to us the meaning of time made new: the *prayer of the Hours*.

Through this prayer the mystery of the liturgy that is celebrated on Sunday permeates and transfigures the time of daily life. But whereas everything is given to us in the liturgy of the Lord's Day, here we give everything back. There everything is grace; here everything becomes praise of the glory of his grace. The "office", the service, of the Bride, is then "divine": her sole occupation is loving. In this office our entire being takes part in praising the Father through his Son in his Holy Spirit. Our "person"—body, soul, spirit, and heart—becomes in its every fiber a prayer, but so does our being "in relation to God", since it is the community that prays, and, finally, our being "in time", since this ongoing mortal time of ours is transformed into an offering by the dew of the Spirit. The office is our incarnate participation in the prayer of Jesus himself. The prayer that the Word makes to the Father expands and, in the form of praise, takes flesh in us who are in synergy with the Holy Spirit. The office is a prism allowing the pure light of the Son's own praise to be channeled through the adopted sons of God.

Understandably, then, the prayer of the Hours consists chiefly of the prayer that Jesus himself used in his mortal condition: the psalms. In this single book of the Old Testament the entire economy of salvation became prayer, and now this love-inspired plan has been fulfilled in Jesus. When the Church prays, the liturgy that "fulfills" this love-inspired plan is expressed through these same psalms. In them the Spirit repeats with the Bride the wonderful deeds of her Lord. The texts that we call the "hymns" of the prayer of the Hours are the blossoming of the psalms as prayed by Christ; they are, as it were, the psalms of the New Covenant. In its litanic prayers the Church voices for "today" the intercession that first found expression in the psalms.

The biblical readings that are at the heart of the office complete the promise of the psalms. We no longer go to meet the Word solely through the prayer of expectation; rather, when we hear the word of God, we encounter the Word in the silence of pure faith: there is nothing to say; we can only receive him in a spirit of utter poverty. At this point, the encounter is not mediated by the prayer of those who were our fathers in the faith; our faith clings directly to him who is its source and goal. When the wind reaches us, it has crossed mountains and valleys, seas and cities; so too the Breath of the Spirit reaches us laden with the redemptive drama of generations past. But when it finally touches us, it causes us to be born directly into the life of the Son and to "see the kingdom of God".

For the office is indeed divine: it is the divine occupation par excellence, the occupation of those who dwell in the kingdom of love. It is relaxation in the spirit, as contrasted with the tensions and "preoccupations" of the world. It transfigures us because it makes "this world as we know it ... pass away" (1 Cor 7:31) and reveal its true nature as a gift. It truly re-creates us by reminding us of the life to which we are called and making us live that life here and now: "Eternal life is this: to know you, the only true God, and Jesus Christ whom you have sent" (Jn 17:3).

Even though the prayer of the heart, which is absolutely indispensable, opens us to all the dimensions of love in human history, the office goes further in one direction: it transcends individuals, taking them out of themselves and making them one in the community. It is then that the Church prays as the Church, the Bride of the Lord of history, moved by the Spirit and surrendered to the Father: "Look, I and the children whom God has given me" (Heb 2:13). The office is the office of a people who are priests in the one Priest, the "compassionate and trustworthy high priest" (Heb 2:17). "He ... made us a kingdom of priests to serve his God and Father: to him, then, be glory and power for ever and ever. Amen" (Rev 1:6).

Chapter 14

The Sacramental Space of the Celebration

Christ is our new time, and it is this that we celebrate in the night of faith until everything is brought to its completion in the light of the day of his coming. He is also our living space, our "new universe" (see Rev 21:5), and it is in him that we celebrate the mysteries of faith until everything has become "a new heaven and a new earth", the place where "God lives among men" (Rev 21:1ff.). Even now he is the mysterious place, "hidden in the Father", in which we sacramentally celebrate the eternal liturgy. But in what sense is this place truly sacramental? How can the space of our world contain the new universe?

"Rabbi, Where Do You Live?" (Jn 1:38)

The economy of salvation that is revealed to us in the Bible and brought to fulfillment in our celebrations is marked from one end to the other by the search for a dwelling place. The first creation already exists under this sign. The earth was inhabitable because God prepared it as a dwelling place for the man whom he loves, but it became hostile as soon as fear took hold of the human heart. It is there that God seeks out man: "Where are you?" (Gen 3:9). The first sign of the unreliability of this dwelling place is that man turns it into a hiding place for his self-centeredness instead of throwing it open for encounter and welcome. Henceforth inhospitable to man in flight from God, it becomes captive to a tragic ambiguity: fruitfulness and death, garden and wilderness, home and exile. In light of this ambiguity the promise that springs from the Father's heart becomes intelligible: it will be a world that is a dwelling place for sons who believe in his love. The ambiguity will be removed, for man will be able to dwell in the land of God only if his heart becomes trusting once again.

Go to "a country which I shall show you", but on one condition: "Leave your country . . . and your father's house" (Gen 12:1). When, after centuries of wandering, exoduses, and exiles, the Son himself became a man, he fulfilled both the promise and the condition: he left his Father and entered this world, but did so in order to lead us and bring us into his Father's house (Jn 13:1ff.; 14:1). The first two disciples had an inkling of this when in response to Jesus' question, which was a veiled call but pregnant with hope, "What do you want?" they asked, "Rabbi, where do you live?" (Jn 1:38). Once the Word became flesh, "he lived among us" (Jn 1:14); once the heart of his Mother had become wholly a dwelling place of faith, the faithful Son dwelt in our land. Then everything began to come back to life. The earth on which man hides himself out of fear, and with death as the result, was to become the space in which he would exist in trust and with life as its fruit.

From his conception to his Ascension Jesus brought to fulfillment this mystery of the dwelling place. He who contains the universe in his all-powerful word is himself contained as a child in his Mother's womb. He who fashioned Adam from the soil is fashioned from the virginal soil of Mary. "The Word who creates the world comes looking for shelter in a cave."[1] The cave, the prototypical human dwelling place, was regarded at a very early date as the symbol of the birthplace of Jesus. But in this place, in which man had once been sheltered from death, he now encounters the author of his life. That is precisely what the myrrhbearing women would discover when Jesus had been laid in the final human cave: the tomb. "Why look among the dead for someone who is alive?" (Lk 24:5). At this point, everything is changed. Space, like time, explodes: it is no longer closed in upon itself but is delivered from death and filled with him who contains all things in his very body. From the empty tomb to the closed doors of the upper room, the same mystery of the new universe begins to manifest itself: the "nonplace" of the risen Christ becomes, through his victory over death, the new space of our universe. Henceforth his Ascension keeps expanding the space of his incorruptible body until it is all in all, and the new creation has been brought to completion. "Look, I am with you always; yes, to the end of time" (Mt 28:20).

The Church, House of God

The church of stone or wood that we enter in order to share in the eternal liturgy is indeed a space within our world; it is set apart, however, because it is a space that the Resurrection has burst open. It is not a space that platonically symbolizes an abstract universe, but a space in which a world delivered from death really dwells. It is there that we celebrate the liturgy by bringing to fulfillment the mystery of the body of Christ. This place of celebration is the place where the

---

[1] Kontakion for the Vigil of Christmas in the Byzantine liturgy.

promise of a dwelling is also fulfilled. The very locale, in its sensible materiality, is the place where Christ brings to fulfillment his promise and the expectation of man, for in this sacramental space the Father's house (Jn 14:2) is thrown open to us. Speaking of the icon of Christ, the Second Council of Nicea tells us, "In Christ himself we contemplate both the inexpressible and that which is represented." [2] But what is a church, as a sacramental space, if not an icon of the body of Christ, of the "whole" Christ? [3]

We had a glimpse of this earlier when we reflected on the Ascension of the Lord [4] as a celebration of the eternal liturgy, for all the actors in the mystery are here present, surrounding the assembly that is here and now celebrating. The space of the church is transfigured; its surfaces with their lively icons open beyond themselves into the space of the coming kingdom; its stones on which the wonders of the mystery of Christ are proclaimed become the living stones of the new Jerusalem. It is because this space is sacramental that the church manifests the Church.

It is clear, however, that we must see this sacramental space through the eyes of faith, or we will sink into a subjective symbolism. But the vision of faith is a focused vision; it has a center, and that center is not only the risen Christ under the sign of the Pantocrator or the life-giving Cross, but also that which is the sign of his being a "nonplace" for death: I mean his tomb. The altar is in effect the point of convergence for all the lines in the space that is the church. It is because of the altar that the space of the church is sacramental. The altar tells us that the body of Christ is no longer

---

[2] Second Council of Nicea, Session 6 (Mansi XIII, 244B).
[3] Saint Augustine.
[4] See chap. 4.

here or there in a mortal place, but is risen and fills everything with its presence. This "nonplace" for death becomes
the place where the paschal sacrifice is offered. That is why
a church is not a "sacred" place in the same sense as the
houses of worship built by religions that are searching for
the godhead. The space of our churches with their icons is a
space that is open to the Lord who is coming, a space that is
both expectant and filled, a space that supports the world
and is drawn to the kingdom; it is the place where the epiclesis of the Spirit occurs and where every offering is transformed into the body of Christ.

The Space of the Body of Christ

All men carry within them the dream of a home. For our
God it is no longer a dream but a promise, and in Jesus the
promise is fulfilled. When we build a church, we carry within
us the desire of providing a house, a home, for him and for
us. But are we sufficiently mindful that when we build a
church the prophecy of Nathan to David is being fulfilled
for us: "It is the Lord who will build a house for you" (see 2
Sam 7)? Jesus said the same in his zeal for his Father's house:
"Destroy this temple, and in three days I will raise it up" (Jn
2:19). This gracious reversal, this passage to a dwelling in which
everything is alive, is precisely the shattering of space that occurs
in the Resurrection of Jesus. In the Resurrection the promise
of a dwelling place is also fulfilled.

Men have always felt their houses, their homes, to be pro-
longations of their own bodies, a kind of second space (after
their garments) for their persons. A house humanizes space,
makes it habitable, makes it personal, so much so that the
architecture of early houses was based on the architecture of

the human body. In Christ the Father performs this marvelous adaptation in a way that is beyond all possible expectations: we become his dwelling place by taking on the form of his Son's body. This configuration is given visible symbolization in cruciform churches: when the people of God assemble there, they take on the form of the crucified Christ who overcame death; when the river of life flows out into the new Jerusalem, it gives birth to trees of life.

The space of a house awaits the presence of its inhabitants and is a sign of the quality of their presence. The sacramental space of a church embodies an entirely new expectation. It is open not only to the assembly that celebrates there but to all who are not yet in it and who are still unaware that their true dwelling place is the body of Christ. This space is a sign not only of the Father who waits and the Spirit who calls, but also of a presence that is unmerited gift, sharing, joy, and peace. Once again, the altar is at the center as place of the cup of salvation and thanksgiving, as table of the banquet of divine love. It is because of the altar that the sacramental space not only is focused and centered but also is in movement, the movement being that of the trinitarian communion wherein the body of Christ expands in self-giving and in praise of God's glory. The search for a dwelling place that began in the first paradise is here completed at the heart of the Blessed Trinity: "Remain in me, as I in you. . . . Remain in my love . . . just as . . . I remain in his [the Father's] love" (Jn 15:4, 9, 10).

Like all the sacramental synergies, the space of our celebrations is in an eschatological condition; that is, in it the kingdom is "already" coming, but the space is given to us precisely because the kingdom is "not yet" fully here. "There is no permanent city for us here; we are looking for the one which is yet to be" (Heb 13:14). The people of God who gather in a church are only pausing there on their exodus journey; the ground they occupy is that on which as pilgrims they set their feet, but as soon as they lift up their eyes, they contemplate their Lord who is coming, along with the holy Mother of God and the cloud of witnesses who are journeying with them. The two levels in the visions of the Apocalypse are reflected in the sacramental space of the liturgical celebration.

Finally, this space is sacramental because it acts as mediator. Not only is it the sign of the new universe that is coming to us and drawing us; it also expresses our response, our faith-inspired cooperation with the energy of the Holy Spirit. In a human house space mediates presence; in that space, all can be themselves, can listen and speak, can see their relatives and be acknowledged by them. In the house of God, this entirely new space enables us, in communion with one another, to be ourselves in the truth of the heart, to listen to the saving Word, to contemplate him and be accepted by him. The silence in which we are wrapped is part of the sacramental space of a church. As silence of the heart, it is our answer to the word that transforms us; as silence of the eyes, it is our self-offering to the light that transfigures us. Then, like the seer on Patmos, and in faith that is increasingly purified, we can "turn around to see who is speaking to us" (see Rev 1:12). The risen Christ, the Word and Icon of the Father, will increasingly become our "new universe". We will be able to depart from the church and the sacramental space without leaving the Lamb who is our temple in the Spirit. Abiding in him—and he in us—we will doubtless cease to celebrate his liturgy, but we will begin to live it.

PART THREE

THE LITURGY LIVED

LITURGY AND LIFE

If the liturgy is the mystery of the river of life that streams from the Father and the Lamb and if it reaches us and draws us when we celebrate it, it does so in order that it may water our entire life and render it fruitful. The eternal liturgy in which the economy of salvation reaches completion "is accomplished" by us in our sacramental celebrations in order that it may in turn be accomplished in us, in the least fibers of our being and of our human community. If we are to be convinced that this claim is true, we must note carefully how the liturgy celebrated differs from the liturgy lived. But we must also become aware of why it is that the Christian liturgy does away with the separation that existed under the Old Covenant between cult or worship and moral life. This awareness will bring us to an understanding of the entirely new unity of celebration and life in the fontal liturgy.

Liturgy Celebrated and Liturgy Lived

When we celebrate the liturgy, we participate in an intense and unique way in the totality of our life, in its adorable Lord, in all the men who achieve a new existence in the communion of the Father, in the world that has been reconciled and in time that has been set free. We truly "live" during the celebration, and what we shall be forever is "already" manifested and tasted in the Spirit. None of us is ever so much himself, nor is the Church so much herself, nor are the universe and history so exalted in hope of glory, as when the liturgy is being celebrated. But these are "moments" of fullness and grace. "Time", with its ongoing gestation and tension, still remains. The liturgy continues therein, under the different face given it by time, and in tribulation and affliction. As long as the veil of death still seems to hide our slow penetration by the life of the risen Christ, we enter into the experience of the liturgy as lived. For we live on in the opaqueness of the last times, during which the race as a whole and individual men have "not yet" passed over into incorruptible life.

This dialectic of "time" and "moments" is also to be seen in the quality of the space within which the liturgy unfolds. In the celebration space is sacramental, but in daily life it seems to be simply a setting for us. The signs that manifest the Christian newness bring this distinction home to us. In celebrations they are so simple and bare that they become immediately transparent to faith, but in daily life everything is circumstantial and needs to be continually discerned and transfigured.

During the "moments" of celebration the intense gift of the Holy Spirit causes us to experience the Church; it manifests the Church, causes her to grow, and transforms her into the body of Christ. During the "time" that is life this gift of communion is no less intense and faithful, but the individuals in the communion find themselves bound by their various ties to the human community. The mystery of God's communion with man then needs to be tested in actuality and by ourselves. We have become the body of Christ: Are we going to live as his body?

In everyday life the synergies of the Holy Spirit and the Church seem to be rather those of the Paraclete and the individual Christian, even if, at a deeper level, they are always the synergies of the body of Christ. In celebrations these synergies are sacramental; they take pedagogical form as a practical mystagogy. In the rest of Christian life, they are unforeseeable and spontaneous, lacking in precise outline, and intermingled with one another. It is no longer possible to distinguish clearly when the Spirit is revealing Jesus to us, when he is transforming us into Jesus, and when he is establishing us in communion with him. It might even seem that of these three synergies, which are so clear in the Eucharist— the liturgy of the word, the anaphora, and the communion— Christian existence focuses chiefly on the third. And in fact, if the celebration is the "moment" of sowing, life is more the "time" for bearing fruit.

Our celebrations regularly end with a blessing, but this "ending" is a sending forth, a mission: let us now live in him whom we have received, and let us share him with others. The celebration has carried us once more into the very heart of the divine agape; with that as our starting point, we must now exercise our manifold gifts and charisms for the good of all. If the Lord of glory has transfigured us, then we must now radiate him in our kenosis. The power of the Spirit has configured us to the crucified body of Jesus; it must now manifest in our mortal flesh the power of his Resurrection.

The Liturgy: Beyond Worship and Moral Life

But why does this carryover not always take place? Why the gap between the wonder of our celebrations and the dullness of a life that is so little Christianized? It is a continual source of surprise to us that we are sinners, but this wretched state is perhaps less the cause than the effect of the separation we maintain between celebration and life. Instead of being surprised that we are sinners, we should ask ourselves whether we have not remained under the regime of the old law, of the "letter" whose characteristic is precisely that it cannot give life (2 Cor 3:6).

The time of the promises is a magnificent one, but it is a time of preevangelization. When the Holy Spirit prefigures Christ in the saving events, his primary purpose is to prepare hearts to receive this Christ. The Spirit's pedagogy is existential. In the presence of God's actions, he calls upon men to bare their hearts and take a stand. Under the Old Covenant the Spirit's pedagogy operated on two distinct and separate levels: cult or worship and moral life.

First, there was cult or public worship. Men, faced with the God who speaks, were taught by their cult to listen and remember. The saving acts of the living God were the basis for this remembering of the heart, and it was to them that the ritual actions referred. Cult became a testimony and even a memorial. The heart that remembered then became a heart that adored and gave thanks, "for his love is everlasting!"

But this testimony of adoration and thanksgiving was to be kept alive and become part of the moral life. The saving events that the heart remembered and the cult memorialized were also guides for action. The whole of Deuteronomy is a plea that the hearts of the Israelites should retain the word of God and put it into practice. The fidelity of believers was to be a response to the fidelity of God, who saves. This response of fidelity was to be the condition for the fulfillment of the promises under the Covenant.

At the same time, however, the time of the promises was only preliturgical. The saving events, like events of the present world, occurred once and then belonged to the past. The heart that kept the word alive in it did indeed remember the events in ritual actions, but the events remained past. The faithful heart that observed the law also remembered them, but they served only as a heteronomous model. We must be clear on this twofold deadly rift from which the religion of the Old Covenant still suffered: its worship did not contain the saving events within it but simply remembered them; its morality aimed at conformity with the events but did not flow from them as from a present source.

The earlier covenants had each its cult—the first, sacrificial; the later, synagogal—but did not as yet have experience of the liturgy. Their worship was the expression of a human religious response. This explains the cultural elements that played such a large part in the temple sacrifices; it explains, too, the cyclical repetitions that marked this cult. The author of the Letter to the Hebrews stresses these symptoms of death that made the temple, the priesthood, and the levitical sacrifices irremediably helpless to bestow life. The mosaic law did indeed serve a pedagogical purpose by developing, on the one hand, a set of cultic rites and, on the other, a religion of the heart, and by requiring that the two become increasingly harmonized with each other. The Old Covenant was nonetheless still marked by a pre-Christian attitude as far as the relation between moral outlook and its cultic expression was concerned: on the one side, the signified; on the other, the signifier. Morality and ritual went hand in hand but remained external to each other. The human person was not integrated. The encounter in depth of gift and reception was still in the future.

During the time from Moses to Jesus there was an inevitable dichotomy between the ritual activity of worship and moral fidelity to the law. Only when "grace and truth" (Jn 1:17) were given by the one Son was this reciprocal exteriority eliminated. For us there are no longer ritual actions *and* interior worship, but a wholly new unity of the two (Jer

31:31–34). Christians are no longer divided between two activities that relate them to their God: sacred actions on certain occasions, secular actions the rest of the time (even if both kinds of action were meant, under the Old Covenant, to be inspired by the same love). "These are only a shadow of what was coming: the reality is the body of Christ" (Col 2:17). The New Covenant takes us beyond the separation of cult and moral life. This "beyond" is liturgy "in spirit and truth" (Jn 4:24).

The Single Mystery of the Liturgy

The liturgy, which is celebrated at certain moments but lived at every moment, is the one mystery of the Christ who gives life to men. When it is celebrated, it does not offer us a model that is then to be imitated in the rest of life; if this were the case, we would be back in the separation of sacred ritual from moral conduct. The Christ whom we celebrate is the identical Christ by whom we live; his mystery permeates both celebration and life. Just as his sacraments are his mysteries, so his life in us is "mystical", or it does not exist at all. His Holy Spirit is the one wellspring from which we drink in the sacramental celebration and which streams in our hearts for eternal life. But without celebration no life is possible, for if we are not filled by the river of life, how can we bear the fruits of the Spirit?

Our wellspring and our life are the great gift of the risen Lord to us. The radical continuity of his energy makes itself felt from the moment of our baptism and chrismation; grafted onto Christ and penetrated by the seal of his Spirit we are able to celebrate and live in its fullness the mystery of life, which the Father bestows on us abundantly. When we are reconciled by the renewed gift of the Spirit, who is in his person the forgiveness of our sins, we are able to "realize" the eucharistic communion and then extend it to the human community. The epiclesis of the body of Christ, of which ordained ministers are the servants, is then communicated to all the members according to the charisms given them by their royal priesthood. The epiclesis in the lives of Christians and through them in the world is the continuing source of the lived liturgy; for then the Spirit who is our life also guides our behavior (Gal 5:25).

Through the kenosis of the suffering members of Christ the eternal liturgy thus permeates our world as a leaven of immortality that causes the last times to "rise" toward their completion and fulfillment. The glory of the ascending Christ does not flash into our time only intermittently; rather it penetrates it continually with its transfiguring power. That is how the wonder that we celebrate becomes life for all men. The celebration teaches us to live by this mystery; our lives take root in the celebration and begin to open and expand. When the kingdom finally comes, the celebration of the mystery and the living of the mystery will be forever one. In that eternity, to live the mystery will be to celebrate it, just as even now to celebrate it is to enter into "the long, eternal day of light" that is life.

Chapter 15

Prayer, the Liturgy of the Heart

The Heart Is Our Place

The outstreaming of the mystery of the liturgy into the rest of life begins in prayer, and the point where the river of life rises as a wellspring in the midst of human existence is the heart. It is through the prayer of the heart that liturgy becomes life. This is the personal threshold that must be crossed and at which everything is decided, but it also represents a call to which we find it hard to respond. If we shrink back, our celebrations once again become mere rites, and the liturgy remains alien to our lives. But if we resolve to pray, humbly and in self-surrender to the Spirit, our entire being descends into our heart and is gathered up in its source. The heart is for us the existential starting point of the entire movement of the liturgy, both celebrated and lived.

We pray as we live, and we live as we love; everything depends on the place that is our habitual focus and around which everything acquires meaning. Is our "place" the biological ego, the social ego, the cerebral ego or world of ideas, the superego, our dreams, and so on? But these are all peripheral dwellings in which we are only visitors; we are not at home in them; while we live in them, we have not yet found ourselves. Only in the heart are we ourselves; only there do we become ourselves. The heart is the place of authentic encounter with ourselves, with others and, above all, with the living God. The heart is not something static, a kind of void to be filled (that is the illusion created by the peripheral dwellings); it is alive: a yearning for a presence and a creative response to a presence. The heart is the place of decision; it is the personal dimension in our "Yes" or "No". It is our very person in its point of origin, its irreducible mystery, its inviolable freedom. We cannot objectivize it, because in the very act in which we examine it, it has already made its choice; it is prior to, and present in, our consciousness of it; it eludes our grasp. It is "toward" another presence, and it suffers the exhaustion of death as long as it finds satiety in objects. In the final analysis, the heart is the man as image of the trinitarian communion and in search of the likeness, that is, of this divine communion. Only this divine presence can be the true life of man, because it alone fills the heart by deepening the heart's desire; it alone does not delude the heart by satiating it but rather expands it by drawing it.

"Where do you live?" (Jn 1:38). The Lord is to be found only where men consent to encounter him. Once we decide to cross the threshold of our own heart, we discover it to be the place where the wellspring sends forth its streams: "Truly, Yahweh is in this place, and I did not know!" (Gen 28:16). There, presence meets presence, and this mysterious hospitality marks the dawning of prayer after our long nights of evasion or drowsiness. For it is our heart that prays, and not our structures (even our psychic structures) or our determinisms or our conditionings. All these are doubtless the space in which we move, but changes in the decor will never substitute for the newness that encounter brings. And encounter takes place only when the heart turns back to him who is, for it is then that he comes.

To Enter into the Name of the Holy Lord Jesus

The movement of prayer is identical with the movement of the liturgy as lived in an impoverished but profound way in the heart. Christian prayer cannot be defined, because the mystery of Christ, which it welcomes and for which it longs, cannot be defined. It stretches between two "ignorances": before the Holy Spirit lays hold of us, "we do not know *how* to pray properly" (Rom 8:26), but once he has brought us into the prayer of Jesus, we will not know *what* we pray *for*: we will simply pray. The celebration of the liturgy can be described because it uses sacramental signs; the liturgy of the heart is as indescribable as the mystery that it lives out. Here the signs have disappeared; all that are left are the root (faith) that gave them their sap and the hope that they promised (namely, love). The mystery, "kept secret for endless ages" (Rom 16:25), increasingly fills the heart that believes and hopes; it becomes there a "silent love".[1]

The Holy Spirit is our pedagogue in prayer, just as he is our mystagogue in celebration. We must begin with and through him; otherwise we shall go astray into barren paraliturgies that do not reach the heart. Here again, everything begins with the liturgy of the word: not a liturgy made up of our verbiage but the liturgy of the Word who has taken our flesh. The beginning of our sacramental celebrations expresses this coming of the Father's word into our humanity, by having the Gospel, that is, Christ, make its way in procession into the community that celebrates him. In the liturgy of the heart the Holy Spirit endeavors constantly, "from beginning to new beginning", to bring the risen Christ into the heart that is awakening to prayer. His energy,

---

[1] Saint John of the Cross.

which is so utterly simple, teaches us to speak by impress-
ing on our "heart of flesh" the one word that expresses
everything: JESUS. Indeed, not only does Jesus come into
us; above all, we enter into him.

Prayer "to" Jesus is our way of genuinely entering into
the liturgy of the heart, because when we call upon Jesus "in
the Holy Spirit" (1 Cor 12:3), we enter into the mystery of
his holy name. Isn't that how he himself teaches us to begin
our prayer: "May your name be held holy"? The only divine
name that our lips and hearts can say in a wholly truthful
way is the name of Jesus. All others, including that of "Father",
are analogies or symbols and always in need of purification.
Only the name of Jesus is true without qualification, and it
gives all the others their meaning, especially that of "Father".
When we call upon Jesus, our hearts open to the only name
that is not a word detached from the person but rather contains the presence it invokes. It is the only name that is not
possessed when pronounced, for it opens the heart by drawing it to him.

Invocation of the name of Jesus is not an optional method,
like the techniques of prayer, which all religions have, or a
variety of ritual, like the manifold liturgies of the Churches.
Rather it is the first movement of the Spirit in the heart of
the Bride: the Bride's entire mission is fulfilled in Jesus, and
if we enter into the name of the Lord, we are on the only
road that leads to the Father. When we enter into the name
of the holy Lord Jesus, the result is much more than the
sudden emotion felt by Moses as he put off his shoes and
approached the burning bush. When we invoke this name,
we are immersed in his mystery; at each breath we live out
our baptism into him; we offer to him all the innermost
recesses of our humanity, which he makes his own, and we
are permeated by his divinity, which he hands over to us.

When the heart calls upon Jesus, the Word "completes" his Incarnation in it and divinizes it, for Jesus is the beloved Son, who became a man in order that men might become sons of God. In him everything is given by the Father, and everything is offered back by man. For he into whom we enter in the loving silence of our hearts is the risen Jesus, the icon of the invisible God, who unites us to his glorious body. Our prayer is focused on his adorable humanity. It is through his glorified flesh that this prayer reaches the bosom of the Father. Our prayer can only be Jesus, the incarnate Word; otherwise it is empty words and lapses back into death.

The Altar of the Heart

The name of Jesus is the new space for the liturgy of prayer. In speaking of the celebration of the liturgy, we saw the importance of the altar as the focal point of sacramental space and of the movement in it. The same holds for the heart in the space of prayer: it is at the center, and it is from it that the entire movement of the mystery starts. Christian prayer is not to be looked for in an emptying of the mind,[2] since the risen Christ is its mysterious space. All of the asceticism that accompanies prayer thus receives its focus. Its aim is not to make persons and things disappear from view; rather it purifies the relationship of the heart to all that exists, so that the heart may be where its treasure—the Lord—is. The decisive question for prayer is not the local or mental space it inhabits, but the presence that dwells in that space. This presence

---

[2] The reader will be familiar with the strong warnings of Saint Thérèse of Jesus in this regard. The spiritual tradition of the Churches, Eastern and Western, holds no brief for techniques aimed at creating a mental void. Therapy, of whatever order, is not yet a way of prayer.

is in the heart as on an altar on which the Holy Spirit places
and engraves the eternal Gospel: Jesus.

For it is on the altar of the heart that this liturgy of pure
faith is celebrated. The tomb is there to which our nostalgic
memories of the Lord drive us and where the Spirit reveals
that he has been raised up. The tomb is there in which prayer
lays the always suffering body of Christ, certain that the author
of life will raise it up. The tomb is there wherein the living
Word descends into our hells in order to deliver us from our
death. For the nights of our prayer are indeed the descent of
the light into the depths of our darkness. Buried once and
for all with Christ, in the prayer of the heart we continually
experience this burial from which we rise up ever more one
with him and ever more alive for the Father.

On the Great Saturday the body of the Son of God rested
in the earth; he had already conquered death but had not yet
been revealed as the risen One. The same holds for the prayer
of the heart. Buried in the silence of the last times, the praying heart destroys death in its own depths, although it does
not yet burst forth in praise of God's glory. Configured thus
to its Lord, the praying heart becomes the "ecclesial soul" of
which Origen speaks. Like the myrrh bearers, it learns from
the Spirit the inventiveness of divine love. The most beautiful service the Church renders to this world is to come to
the tomb and to stand at the altar of the heart, not now to
embalm the body of Jesus but to heal the dead who throng
the earth by offering them even now the hope and pledge of
the Resurrection. The "silent love" of prayer "to" Jesus then
expands into its proper space, for it gives life to the members
of Jesus who are wounded by death, and it is the place in his
body from which love spreads. When we pray thus in the
Spirit, the name of Jesus is "poured out" (Song 1:3) over his
crucified body. We are then the Church in her most hidden

but also most life-giving mystery: we are at the heart of the kenosis of the Spirit and the Bride.

The Epiclesis of the Heart

In sacramental celebrations the decisive synergy of the Spirit and the Church is exercised at the moment of the epiclesis. As the moment when the silence of the Church is thickest and the might of the Spirit is most intense, the epiclesis is pure prayer and sovereign power: in response to the gift of utterly naked faith comes the virginal gift of the Holy Spirit, and as a result everything in the body of Christ is raised to life. In ongoing life the liturgy of the heart actualizes this marvelous deed, which God accomplishes in the celebration. It is there that the royal priesthood of the baptized is lived primarily and most intensely. The seal of the gift of the Spirit, received once and for all in chrismation, then makes us priests of the New Covenant. On the altar of our hearts we can offer everything—and if we offer little it is because we are still "of little faith"—but the Spirit will transform only what we offer to him. This is the mysterious synergy of prayer: that the more our will is submissive to that of the Father, the more the Father does our will! That is the prayer of the saints, because from the moment that he assumed a human will that is how the Lord Jesus prayed. It is in the epiclesis of the heart that all Christian holiness is determined at its source, namely, the straightened yet confident and resolute faith of sinners who resign their own wills into the hands of the Father and thus draw down the superabundant gift of a love that is poured out in their hearts. The more the heart is stripped of all attachments, the more it is filled by the Spirit; the more humble and trusting the silence, the more the name of Jesus expands it with its presence.

It is this holiness that we fear when our old self flees prayer; we abandon the altar of the heart and maintain that we are exercising our "royal" priesthood by working on the structures of the present world, as if structures could cause the "kingdom" to come! This basic temptation reveals something more to us about the mystery of prayer: for what we really fear is having to come face to face with death. The drama of death, as we have seen, is at the bottom of the mystery of the epiclesis. But when the heart resolves to pray, it enters into the kenosis of the Spirit and the Bride; it shares in the epiclesis of the Church and is posted in the van of the great struggle, the great paschal combat. Prayer is a combat in which the Spirit strengthens us as we fight: he takes away our pathetic weapons, leaving us like young David, and then clads us in the armor of the Son of David and gives us the weapons of the Cross. Prayer is no longer the festive celebration of the Eucharist; all the signs have vanished, and it is in the depths of night that silent love wins the victory over death. This victory is given not only to those who pray but also to all who lie prostrate in the darkness of sin, for these too share in the decisive moment of the epiclesis. Such is the prayer of the saints that allows the world to survive in hope. It is thus that the Lord comes through the patience of his saints.

The Altar of Communion

If the heart perseveres, no matter what the cost, in invoking its Lord Jesus, it will experience the baptism of tears, which cleanses it of its sins; then it will experience the baptism of fire, the baptism of that love into which the Spirit plunges it in the epiclesis of faith. The Holy Spirit will have so fused the rebellious will with the will of the Father that prayer "to" Jesus will have become the prayer "of" Jesus himself. But this ceaseless prayer of Jesus is identical with the eternal liturgy that he celebrates before the face of the Father. The same Spirit who taught us to breathe the name of Jesus will then be able to open us, in the very prayer of Jesus himself, to wonder-filled adoration: "Abba, Father!" When the fontal liturgy wells up in the heart, it expands into "worship in spirit and in truth" (Jn 4:14 and 24). And the epiclesis of the heart expands into an epiclesis over the world; this in turn is naught else than a participation in the great "work" (Jn 5:17) of Christ in his Ascension: that is, the pouring out of the Holy Spirit into the hearts of men in order to draw them to himself.

The praying heart discovers that its true space is the ongoing event of the Ascension. In all honesty, however, we must admit that this is not the space our hearts consciously inhabit. But if we stop with this admission, it is because we have not yet grasped the wonder of the humanity of Jesus, which is woven precisely of our humanity and that of all men. When our interior horizon, which is inseparable from that of others, is filled with sadness, why do we not acknowledge the bond of mortal flesh that makes us one with so many other hopeless and loveless men? Yet this fiber of our humanity is no longer simply our own but belongs also to him who has assumed it and who died and rose for us. The same holds for the least clouds and for the wonderful light that make up our world. In the liturgy of the heart the space of prayer is now never closed off and turned in on itself but is open and spread out, in communion with a multitude of others, and drawn into the horizonless space of him who is Lord of our lives.

For the altar of the heart is in the end the banquet table at which the communion of the Blessed Trinity is constantly given to us in the body of Christ, but given in order that we may share it with others. As meeting place of God's desire and human hunger, the praying heart shares the expectation of the poor and the superabundant gifts of the Father. It is present at the banquet table of love, less in the festivity of the eucharistic meal than in the painful hope of those who do not yet share in it. Thanks to the prayers of the saints, no one is left outside. For what the prayer of pure faith and silent love celebrates is the hidden depths of eucharistic communion; it immerses itself in the depths of the last times in order to call to the feast of wisdom the foolish men who turn away from it.

Here is located the true fasting of those who willingly persevere in prayer: they sit at the table of hungry sinners. Prayer then makes its own the desire of the beloved Son, who came to share with others the paschal meal at which he gives himself. But who shall ever be capable of singing the joy of the Holy Spirit, the great Hallel of this mysterious banquet? For the more a heart consents to this kind of prayer, the more the Spirit unites himself with it in the kenosis of love. The liturgy of prayer is increasingly a source of life for a multitude to the extent that the heart is handed over to the Spirit in peace, that peace which is the power of the resurrection at work in the depths of death. The heart that prays in this way will increasingly be drawn by its Lord into his life-giving Ascension; but will it be able to go any further, inasmuch as when it reaches the boundary of death the Spirit has already brought it to the furthest love can go (see Jn 13:1)?

Chapter 16

The Divinization of Man

If we consent in prayer to be flooded by the river of life, our entire being will be transformed; we will become trees of life and be increasingly able to produce the fruit of the Spirit: we will love with the very Love that is our God. It is necessary at every moment to insist on this radical consent, this decision of the heart by which our will submits unconditionally to the energy of the Holy Spirit; otherwise we shall remain subject to the illusion created by mere knowledge of God and talk about him and shall in fact remain apart from him in brokenness and death. On the other hand, if we do constantly renew this offering of our sinful hearts, let us not imagine that our New Covenant with Jesus will be a personal encounter pure and simple. The communion into which the Spirit leads us is not limited to a face-to-face encounter between the person of Christ and our own person or to an external conformity of our wills with his. The lived liturgy does indeed begin with this "moral" union, but it goes much further. The Holy Spirit is an anointing, and he seeks to transform all that we are into Christ: body, soul, spirit, heart, flesh, relations with others and the world. If love is to become our life, it is not enough for it to touch the core of our person; it must also impregnate our entire nature.

To this transformative power of the river of life that permeates the entire being (person and nature), the undivided tradition of the Churches gives an astonishing name that sums up the mystery of the lived liturgy: *theosis* or divinization. Through baptism and the seal of the gift of the Holy Spirit we have become "sharers of the divine nature" (2 Pet 1:4). In the liturgy of the heart, the wellspring of this divinization streams out as the Holy Spirit, and our individual persons converge in a single origin. But how is this mysterious synergy to infuse our entire nature from its smallest recesses to its most obvious behaviors? This process is the drama of divinization in which the mystery of the lived liturgy is brought to completion in each Christian.

The Mystery of Jesus

To enter into the name of the holy Lord Jesus does not mean simply contemplating it from time to time or occasionally identifying with his passionate love for the Father and his compassion for men. It also means sharing faithfully and increasingly in his humanity, in assuming which he assumed ours as well. In our baptism we "put on Christ" in order that this putting on might become the very substance of our life. The beloved Son has united us to himself in his body, and the more he makes our humanity like his own, the more he causes us to share in his divinity. The humanity of Jesus is new because it is holy. Even in its mortal state it shared in the divine energies of the Word, without confusion and in an unfathomable synergy in which his will and human behavior played their part. Jesus is not a divinized man; he is the truly incarnated Word of God.

This last statement means that we need not imitate, from afar and in an external way, the behavior of Jesus as recorded in the Gospel, in order thereby to effect our own divinization

and become "like God"; self-divinization is the primal temptation ever lurking in wait. On the contrary, it is the Word
who divinizes this human nature, which he has united to
himself once and for all. Since his Resurrection his divine-
human energies are those of his Holy Spirit, who elicits and
calls for our response; in the measure of this synergy of the
Spirit and our heart our humanity shares in the life of the
holy humanity of Christ. To enter into the name of Jesus,
Son of God and Lord, means therefore to be drawn into him
in the very depths of our being, by the same drawing movement in which he assumed our humanity by taking flesh and
living out our human condition even to the point of dying.
There is no "panchristic" pseudo-mysticism here, because
the human person remains itself, a creature who is free over
against its Lord and God. Neither, however, is there any moralism (a further error that waits to ensnare us), because our
human nature really shares in the divinity of its Savior.

"Man becomes God as much as God becomes a man",
says Saint Maximus the Confessor.[1] Christian holiness is divinization because in our concrete humanity we share in the
divinity of the Word who married our flesh. The "divine
nature" of which Saint Peter speaks (2 Pet 1:4) is not an
abstraction or a model, but the very life of the Father, which
he eternally communicates to his Son and his Holy Spirit.
The Father is its source, and the Son extends it to us by
becoming a man. We become God by being more and more
united to the humanity of Jesus. The only question left, then—
since this humanity is the way by which our humanity will
put on his divinity—is this: How did the Son of God live as
a man in our mortal condition? The Gospel has been written precisely in order to show us "the mind of Christ Jesus"

[1] PG 91:101C.

(Phil 2:5);[2] it is this mind with which the Holy Spirit seeks to fill our hearts.

According to the spirituality of the Church and according to the gifts of the Spirit given to every one, each of the baptized lives out more intensely one or other aspect of the mind of Christ; at the same time, however, the mystery of divinization is fundamentally the same in all Christians. Their humanity no longer belongs to them, in the possessive and deadly sense of "belong", but to him who died and rose for them. In an utterly true sense, all that makes up my nature—its powers of life and death, its gifts and experiences, its limits and sins—is no longer "mine" but belongs to "him who loved me and gave himself up for me". This transfer of ownership is not idealistic or moral but realistic and mystical. As we shall see, the identification of Jesus with the humanity of every human person plays a very large part in the new relationship that persons establish with other men; but when the identification is willingly accepted and when our rebellious wills submit to his Spirit, divinization is at work. I was wounded by sin and radically incapable of loving; now Love has become part of my nature again: "I am alive; yet it is no longer I, but Christ living in me" (Gal 2:20).

The Realism of the Liturgy of the Heart

The mystical realism of our divinization is the fruit of the sacramental realism of the liturgy. Conversely, evangelical

---

[2] Sometimes translated as "the sentiments of Christ Jesus". The meaning, however, is not "sentiments" in an emotional sense, but rather attitudes of the heart that lead to certain forms of behavior, that is, the "ways of God" lived at the human level.

moralism, with which we so often confuse life according to the Spirit, is the inevitable result of a deterioration of the liturgy into sacred routines. But when the fontal liturgy, which is the realism of the mystery of Christ, gives life to our sacramental celebrations, in the same measure the Spirit transfigures us in Christ.

The Fathers of the early centuries tell us that "the Son of God became a man, in order that men might become sons of God". The stages by which the beloved Son came among us and united himself to us to the point of dying our death are the same stages by which he unites us to him and leads us to the Father, to the point of making us live his life. These stages of the one Way that is Christ are shown to us in figures in the Old Testament; Jesus fulfilled the prefigurations. The stages are creation and promise, Passover and exodus, Covenant and kingdom, exile and return, restoration and expectation of the consummation. The two Testaments inscribed this great Passover of the divinizing Incarnation in the book of history. But in the last times the Bible becomes life; it exists in a liturgical condition, and the action of God is inscribed in our hearts. Knowledge of the mystery is no longer a mental process but an event that the Holy Spirit accomplishes in the celebrated liturgy and then brings to fulfillment by divinizing us.

But it is not enough simply to understand the ways in which Christ divinizes us; the primary thing is to be able to live them. At certain "moments" the celebrated liturgy gives us an intense experience of the economy of salvation, which is divinization, in order that we may live it at all "times", these new times into which it has brought us. According to the Fathers of the desert, either we pray always or we never pray. But in order to pray always we must pray often and sometimes at length. In like manner (for we are dealing with the same mystery), in order to divinize us the Spirit must divinize us often and sometimes very intensely. The economy of salvation that emerges from the Father through his Christ in the Holy Spirit expands to become the divinized life that Christians live in the Holy Spirit, through the name of Jesus, the Christ and Lord, in movement toward the Father. But the celebration of the liturgy is the place and moment in which the river of life, hidden in the economy, penetrates the life of the baptized in order to divinize it. It is there that everything that the Word experiences for the sake of man becomes Spirit and life.

The Holy Spirit, Iconographer of Divinization

In the economy of salvation everything reaches completion in Jesus through the outpouring of the Holy Spirit; in the liturgy as celebrated and as lived everything begins through the Holy Spirit. That is why at the existential origin of our divinization is the liturgy of the heart, the synergy in which the Holy Spirit unites himself to our spirit (Rom 8:16) in order to make us be, and show that we are, sons of God. The same Spirit who "anointed" the Word with our humanity and imprinted our nature upon him is written in our hearts as the living seal of the promise, in order that he may "anoint" us with the divine nature: he makes us christs in Christ. Our divinization is not passively imposed on us, but is our own vital activity, proceeding inseparably from him and from ourselves.

When the Spirit begins his work in us and with us, he is not faced with the raw, passive earth out of that he fashioned the first Adam or, much less, the virginal earth, permeated by faith, that he used in effecting the conception of the second Adam. What the Spirit finds is a remnant of glory, an icon of the Son: ceaselessly loved, but broken and disfigured. Each of us can whisper to him what the funeral liturgy cries out in the name of the dead person: "I remain the image of your inexpressible glory, even though I am wounded by sin!" [3] This trust that cannot be confounded and this Covenant that cannot be broken form the space wherein the patient mystery of our divinization is worked out.

The sciences provide grills for interpreting the human riddle, but when these have been applied three great questions still remain in all that we seek and in all that we do: the search for our origin, the quest for dialogue, the aspiration for communion. On the one hand, why is it that I am what I am, in obedience to a law that is stronger than I am (see Rom 7) ? On the other, in the smallest of my actions I await a word, a counterpart who will dialogue with me. Finally, it is clear that our mysterious selves cannot achieve fulfillment on any level, from the most organic to the most aesthetic, except in communion. These three pathways in my being are, as it were, the primary imprints in me of the image of glory, of the call of my very being to the divine likeness in which my divinization will be completed. The Holy Spirit uses arrows of fire in restoring our disfigured image. The fire of love consumes its opposite (sin) and transforms us into itself, which is Light.

We wander astray like orphans as long as we have not accepted him, the Spirit of sonship, as our virginal source. All burdens are laid upon us, and we are slaves as long as we are not surrendered to him who is freedom and grace. And because he is the Breath of Life, it is he who will teach us to listen (we are dumb only because we are deaf); then, the

[3] Byzantine funeral liturgy.

more we learn to hear the Word, the better we shall be able to speak. Our consciences will no longer be closed or asleep, but will be transformed into creative silence. Finally, Utopian love and the communion that cannot be found because it is "not of this world" are present in him, the "treasure of every blessing", not as acquired and possessed but as pure gift; our relationship with others becomes transparent once again. This communion of the Holy Spirit is the master stroke in the work of divinization, because in this communion we are in communion also with the Father and his Son, Jesus (2 Cor 13:13; Jn 1:3), and with all our brothers.

Following these three pathways of the transfigured icon, we are divinized to the extent that the least impulses of our nature find fulfillment in the communion of the Blessed Trinity. We then "live" by the Spirit, in oneness with Christ, for the Father. The only obstacle is possessiveness, the focusing of our persons on the demands of our nature, and this is sin, for the quest of self breaks the relation with God. The asceticism that is essential to our divinization and that represents once again a synergy of grace consists in simply but resolutely turning every movement toward possessiveness into an offering. The epiclesis on the altar of the heart must be intense at these moments, so that the Holy Spirit may touch and consume our death and the sin that is death's sting. Entering into the name of Jesus, the Son of God and the Lord who shows mercy to us sinners, means handing over to him our wounded nature, which he does not change by assuming but which he divinizes by putting on. From offertory to epiclesis and from epiclesis to communion the Spirit can then ceaselessly divinize us; our life becomes a eucharist until the icon is completely transformed into him who is the splendor of the Father.

Chapter 17

The Liturgy in Work and Culture

The Unrecognized Iconography

Many a reader will be surprised to read, immediately after chapters on the prayer of the heart and human divinization, a chapter on work and culture as experiences of the lived liturgy. But the surprise is itself revelatory of the mystery of the liturgy. The imperfectly spiritual persons that we sometimes are have, strictly speaking, a sense of the vital continuity between liturgical celebration and the new life of the Spirit that moves outward from the heart to embrace our whole being. But work? Have we not learned to contrast Martha and Mary? And if we must harmonize the two in our lives, do not the concessions made to Martha detract from "the better part" that has been chosen by her sister?[1] The carnal persons that we often are do not ask so many questions, because they assume in advance that the liturgy can have nothing to do with what they call life. In both cases, the connection has been broken between man and the earth, between man and the Lord: How, then, he asks, can a single current of life run through man, the universe, and God?

---

[1] Lk 10:38–42. Sound exegesis has tried in vain to restore the precise meaning of this passage; the old dichotomy action/contemplation, improperly applied to this passage, clings hard to life.

The new thing that the liturgy accomplishes is the resto-ration of this wonderful oneness of life. The river that streams from the throne of God and the Lamb is "crystal clear", but carnal men do not see it, and spiritual men discover it only after a lengthy impregnation of the heart, as they learn to act in God and like God. For the liturgy is action: the work of God and the human person in all the dimensions of man. Starting with the heart of the person being divinized, it unfolds in "gifts" and "services" and "activities" (see 1 Cor 12:4–7) whereby everything is made subject to Christ and trans-formed into him. "All belong to you; but you belong to Christ and Christ belongs to God" (1 Cor 3:22–23): such is the great movement of "service" whereby the liturgy seeks its completion in us. The world reflects God's glory; man is his living icon; and his likeness is restored to us in Christ. Human work and culture have their place in this flow of glory.

Work and culture are the place where men and the world meet in the glory of God. This encounter fails or is obscured to the extent that men "lack God's glory" (Rom 3:23). If the universe is to be recognized and experienced as filled with his glory (see Is 6:3), men must first become once again the dwelling places of this glory and be clothed in it; that is why, existentially, everything begins with the liturgy of the heart and the divinization of the human person. We deal in abstrac-tions when we say that a man is a microcosm, and we delude ourselves when we hope that man can divinize his world—as long as it has not become clear that God's glory is the source of the divinization. The glory of the Trinity is lost from sight in its kenosis in creation; it pierces the silence as a tragic call in the human person who is created in the image of that glory. But only in Christ crucified and risen is the seal on history broken and the stream of glory allowed to return to its source. At this point the liturgy is at work. Moreover, the

restoration of God's glory in man and through him in the
universe requires work; this work in turn is still the marvelous doing of the Holy Spirit, the iconographer of the whole
Christ.

The iconography of the Spirit goes unrecognized as long
as creation is held captive (Rom 8:19–22) and cut off from
men by him who "throws himself across the path" [2] and whose
disruptive action passes through the human heart. It is because
the faces of men are bowed to the earth that the earth is
hidden; when in Christ these faces turn to him who is their
glory, the earth can then produce its fruit of light. For men
are of the earth and are the finest fruit the earth promises,
but the seed of the promise is in God and cannot flower
unless men give their consent. For it is in them that the earth
is filled with promise, and it is upon their deliverance that
the earth waits in order to become "a new earth and a new
heaven", a land that is "wedded" and will bring forth "love
and loyalty" (Is 62:4; Ps 85:10–14). The destiny of the cosmos
in the last times thus depends on human work and culture.
Within creation that is still held captive a new creation (Rev
21:5) is in gestation; the Church is "in travail". The Spirit
divinizes men, not simply so that they in turn may humanize
the world (for this by itself is simply a trite variation on the
theme of death), but also and above all so that creation and
men may attain to the freedom of the glory of God.

Work Transfigured

The iconographical work of the Spirit is one of imprinting
and giving light. To the extent that he imprints in us "the

---

[2] The etymological meaning of dia-bolos, devil.

features of Jesus Christ crucified" (see Gal 3:1), he transforms us from light to light; he transfigures us. But human work too is one of imprinting. The human spirit "expresses" itself in the nature that it transforms. A great deal of silence is required in order to rediscover the beauty of the human hand and, consequently, of the tools that are extensions of the hand and diversify the application of its power and sensitivity. On everything that men touch they leave their personal imprint. In this sense, contrary to the romantic view according to which men project themselves into nature, human work awakens nature to the world of the spirit. That which finds expression in the humanization of matter is infinitely more than a purpose or a technique; the fruit of work is the extension of the reign of man, something that cannot be given a quantitative or exchange value. But is this work of imprinting and mastery necessarily a work of light as well? Here is where human work reveals all of its ambiguity: Is it for life or for death?

The age-old mistake of the various idolatries, even the most recent, is to believe that in the drama in which work struggles between life and death, deliverance comes from nature.[3] Yes, creation is indeed innocent and sound, for it presents man with the kenosis of the first love shown by God. At the same time, however, creation groans while awaiting its deliverance, and it is for man to liberate it by becoming free himself. The mistake of the idolatries is to diagnose the struggle while being ignorant of the cause of the evil, namely, the sin that dwells in human hearts. This is why the iconography of the Spirit consists in transfiguring the hearts of men in their work. Living light never comes from outside; it

---

[3] From this point of view, Marxism and capitalism alike are modern versions of the ancient nature religions.

cannot be apprehended; it streams from the heart and is shed from within on the whole person. The glory of God, which is held captive in creation by human sin, can radiate only when the heart of man adapts itself to the light from within. No other course is possible. *Homo faber* is a slave as long as he has not become *homo liturgicus*. If the river of life has not made its way into the heart, how can it make its way into the field of work?

"My Father still goes on working, and I am at work, too" (Jn 5:17). In the case of Christians who have celebrated the Eucharist, the experience of work being transfigured is not the result of a pious imagination; it is utterly real. These know from experience that the power of their risen Lord is at work, freeing their toil from the weight of death. It does so not to spare them labor (the cross is always the hour of decisive toil) but to open up their labor and make it an offering to the Spirit of life. In the heart of the worker, and not in the material reality of what is done, work is again the place of epiclesis. For, whatever we do, both the activity and the product are incomplete as long as they have not been penetrated by the power of the Spirit that carries them beyond death and turns them into a work of light. If the baptized do not experience this in their labors, what are they going to offer up on the altar of the Eucharist? What we offer at the threshold of the anaphora is not gifts but an incompleteness, an appeal (the epiclesis is a groaning), the anxious expectation of creation that carries the imprint of our hands but not yet the imprint of the light.

For this light that transfigures both work and the created thing that work shapes is the light of communion. Like the eucharistic liturgy, the Eucharist as lived out in daily life is crowned by communion. At bottom, it is the absence of this communion that is at the root of injustices in the workplace, with its alienating structures, and of disorders in the economy. The liturgy does not do away with the need for our inventiveness in dealing with these problems. However, it does something even better: since it is not a structure but the Breath of the Spirit, it is prophetic; it discerns; it challenges; it spurs creativity and is translated into actions. It cries out for justice and is the servant of peace. It incites to sharing, for since all the earth belongs to God, the fruit of human labor is meant for all the sons of God. Sharing is the "jubilee year" of work,[4] and Sunday, the day of abstention from activity, is the day on which all work is restored to its purity through gratuitousness; laborious work is for the sake of bread, and Sunday bread, "the bread of this day", is for the sake of the transfiguration of work.

The Iconography of Culture

There is culture and there is culture. Many mean by "culture" only a product of power exercised: the power of a society's prevailing values; or else a body of knowledge patiently gathered and skillfully set forth; or, in the lowest estimate, a know-how. But "culture" can also be understood in its original, dynamic meaning: the transformation of nature by human hands and its impregnation by the mind, with space becoming a dwelling place and the silence of the void the silence of the word. Then earth and men join in toil, although not all toil is automatically transformative; "culture" is attained only when nature is humanized and when men themselves thereby become more human.

---

[4] See Lev 25 and the theological reasons for the sabbatical year and the year of jubilee.

"Anticulture", in contrast, does not make its entrance on the scene only at the point when aesthetes begin to be alarmed; it is at work, like weeds in a cultivated field, as soon as men turn away from their divine vocation, or brute animality suffocates the *logos* in them, or the lies of their demons quench the Spirit. The drama of culture is the drama of men as created creators, as nature rooted in the cosmos but called to bear fruit in communion with God. Shall the river of life save a culture from the barrenness of death?

For culture—or, in other words, the integral calling of men as they move toward the harvest of the kingdom—is not simply creative; it also exists as either fallen or redeemed. No work of culture is innocent. Art, no matter what the claims made for it, is not immediately divine. If beauty is to save the world, it must first cleanse the world. If the work of artisan or artist is to reveal the glory resident in beauty and bring it to fulfillment, it must first have passed through the fire in which creation is restored to its integrity. It is in this fountainhead that the river of life enters into and permeates culture. Culture is an iconography of the Spirit and man, or it is the beauty solely of the devil.

The reason for this is that in its first synergy the work of culture is revelatory. Even though artisans may not be aware of the Spirit who is illumining them, their work is an attempt to bring to light the glory of God that is buried and held captive in creation. In the pottery they fashion, in the children whom they awaken to freedom, in the poem to which they give birth, men who work upon creation are trying to reveal the meaning of a vast symphony in which they are both indispensable instruments and wonder-filled spectators. They are searching for a beloved Face that calls to them from the depths of their being. Here the original condition for all creative and liberating culture becomes clear: a silence, thanks to which men put themselves in tune with the "word-less" Word, the Son who became a "nonspeaker" (an *in-fans*), the "seeds of the Word" that await them in the universe. But the hour when culture dawns is the very hour of creation itself: mute nature is transformed into word, raw matter is impregnated with spirit, opaqueness becomes transparent. Those who allow themselves to be apprehended by the transforming energy of the Holy Spirit then experience a real transfiguration of culture. The supreme activity of man is to consent to a marriage with the Word. If our gaze is to liberate the beauty hidden in all things, it must first be bathed with light in him whose gaze sends beauty streaming out. If our words are to express the symphony of the Word, they must first be immersed in the silence and harmony of the Word. If our hands are to fashion the icon of creation, we must first allow ourselves to be fashioned by him who unites our flesh to the splendor of the Father.

It is then that culture bears its promised fruit, as it anticipates the eternal communion in the lowliness of the flesh. It achieves its goal only when in its own mysterious way it moves man toward communion with God and thereby with reconciled humanity and with nature that has become transparent. The freshness of the first creation, which nostalgically inspires artistic creativity, is no longer in a mythical past but in the world that is coming, and culture, delivered from its bonds, already opens us to that new world. Silence, "the mystery of the world that is coming",[5] transfigures our gaze; we are able to see the glory of God with open eyes. The silence of the eyes, which is as it were the brightness shining from a heart at peace, can then welcome him who comes: yes, "the Word became flesh, and we saw his glory" (Jn 1:14).

[5] Saint Isaac of Nineveh.

Chapter 18

The Liturgy in the Human Community

What is said of the growth of persons and their work must also be said of human relations: either our life is ruled by one or other morality and by nothing more, or it is seized and transfigured by the mystery of Christ. Every moral law, whether of conscience or of Moses (see Rom 2:1–3:20) or even of the Gospel, to the extent that it is reduced to a rule of life, suffers from a congenital inadequacy. It presents itself to conscience as desirable or mandatory, but it is distinct from the will that is to follow or reject it. It reveals our brokenness and sinfulness but does not heal them. There is a heteronomy between the law with its demands and the consenting heart: the heart is a vital principle, the law is only the statement of an ideal. The realism of the liturgy, both celebrated and lived, consists in making the ideal become a vital principle; the Holy Spirit and the human heart then become a source of life, and we are confronted again with the mystery of the synergy, the unparalleled Christian novelty.

After having been formed by the law as by a pedagogue external to themselves, the baptized reach a certain degree of maturity and there find themselves faced with the call addressed to the rich young man: either to be content with the law and to go on constructing their own little perfection or to go further and lose themselves in Christ by handing their hearts over to the power of the Holy Spirit. It is when they choose to go further that they enter into the mystery and are "apprehended by it" (see Phil 3:12). This passage from law to grace, from a deadly moral life to a "mystical" life of conformity to Christ, is always the moment when the river of life crosses a new barrier. Every time that we fall back into our moralism with its promise of security, we dam up the energy of the Holy Spirit; the liturgy is then cut off from the life that it ought to be watering. At each stage of their growth the baptized must choose: either a humanism in which man is the measure of everything, or the liturgy through which the mystery transfigures and divinizes us.

This ongoing drama is especially visible at the level of life in society. Society is not reducible to a set of structures within which relations between men, from the familial to the political, grow and develop; it is also controlled by a set of values, whether unconscious or codified, that inspire human behavior. Social life is both organized and ethical; structures and culture constantly interact in harmony or in opposition. The mystery of Christ is to be introduced into this social life, but in a paradoxical way: the body of Christ in which a new relationship is established among men is not a structure, and the Holy Spirit who is the soul of this new relationship is not a value. We can therefore see how Christians who want to be Christian will get involved in their society in either of two ways: they will confine themselves in the enclosed field of an evangelical humanism, or they will allow the river of life to become the source of an integrated life.

If they make the first choice, the temptation of moralism to which they have succumbed will lead to one or other of two endeavors. The first attempts to set up specifically Christian structures in society, as if the body of Christ were itself a new structure amid the present world. The second tries to extract a social program from the Gospel, as though the Holy

Spirit were reducible to the values of justice and charity. Neither of these approaches will be ineffective at the organizational and ethical levels of social life, but do they completely exhaust the newness of the mystery that is buried like yeast in human societies? We may ask ourselves why it is that the royal priesthood of the baptized, which is so creative at the level of direct personal relationships, is sometimes stricken with spiritual barrenness as soon as Christians enter the arena of social life. We must also take note of the fact that in some types of society the establishment of so-called Christian structures is impossible and that Christian social teachings can have no impact. These two considerations compel us to look further. At what point, then, does the river of life make its way into our human societies? How does the celebrated liturgy become a lived liturgy, a new vital principle for the societal life of Christians? This brings us to the second of the two kinds of involvement mentioned at the end of the preceding paragraph.

"The Kingdom of God Is among You" (Lk 17:21)

The perspective of the eternal liturgy penetrating into our human societies, from the family to the international community, is the perspective of the kingdom. It is here that the energy of the Holy Spirit reveals Christ to us in all the dimensions of human life.

Moralistic Christians think of their social life as a fact and of the kingdom proclaimed by the Gospel as an ideal. The lived liturgy inverts this outlook: the kingdom is a fact; community among men is an ideal. The fullness that is Christ is indeed buried like yeast in the dough of our last times, and yet his coming kingdom is the event that is already at work,

as it were, kneading our societies. "The coming of the kingdom of God does not admit of observation, and there will
be no one to say, 'Look, it is here! Look, it is there!'" as
though it consisted of human groups molded by structures
and culture. Rather, "it is among you".[1] Human community is still an unattained goal at the level of the couple, the
nation, and the world, but the kingdom of God is already
here, really present, as the great presence of God's love to man.

The baptized acknowledge and believe in this very real
gift; above all, they receive it when they celebrate the Eucharist. The novelty of the liturgy, which they live out in society, is that the communion of the kingdom no longer exists
only at the end of the celebration but is also the source of
their presence "among" their fellow men. The disciples of
the earthly Jesus formed a human group, a "society" of believers in Christ; but when the Holy Spirit had been given to
them, they became a community of men and women whose
life was communion with God. At that point the Church
came into existence and, with and in her, the last times. The
irruption of the kingdom of the Holy Spirit into a human
group was thus the event that established authentic community among persons. "Where charity and love are found, there
is God."[2]

By means of this first energy the Holy Spirit reveals to us
the Lord who is and who is coming, and he makes known to
the baptized the ambiguities of their life in society. For our
societies, whatever their extension, are not innocent enti-
ties. The analyses sociologists offer of society, like those that

----

[1] The words that accompany the kiss of peace in the Byzantine liturgy are
"Christ is in our midst, now and for ever."

[2] Antiphon ("Ubi caritas et amor, ibi Deus est") formerly used during the
washing of the feet in the Latin liturgy for Holy Thursday, now used as an
antiphon for the procession with the gifts in the same Mass.

psychoanalysts offer of the soul, are illusory because they seem to provide a cure when in fact they do not know the evil to be healed. The light shed by the kingdom does not claim to replace those analyses, but it does carry the diagnosis further. It shows that throughout the social body there exists a rudimentary possibility of communion, the seeds of community, an appeal for solidarity, a vocation to creative peace. But this same light also unmasks the lie inherent in power, the turning of service into domination, the perverted change of groups into unjust structures, the enslavement of persons to the idol of money. In short, it shows us that society as a whole is an icon of the kingdom. Against a background of glory in which the faithful gift of the Blessed Trinity is constantly manifested, the connecting lines are broken, and the light is obscured. It is because the kingdom of God is "among us" that we can discern the world's true features amid its tragic ambiguity: the world is loved by God, but it is also in the power of the evil one. The lived liturgy impresses on social life the iconography of the person and its culture; it aims at restoring the communion of the kingdom to human groups.

The Church in a State of Epiclesis

The transforming energy of the Holy Spirit operates, as we have seen, in the sacramental epiclesis. It continues to operate in the lived liturgy, at least if we cooperate with it. But if we forget it, we behave as individualists, and this is why the salt loses its savor. When man shared in the divine communion for the first time amid the Babel of the world, the Holy Spirit was given, and he in turn effected the coming of the

Church. When communities living by the divine communion desire to extend this communion to the environments in which they live, what other first step can they take except to present the human groups in which they live for the outpouring of the Holy Spirit? It is then that the kingdom comes through the Church. This epiclesis of the lived liturgy extends the eucharistic epiclesis to our societies. Apart from this ecclesial Pentecost there are only variations on the theme of Babel.

For the other side of our ingenuous humanism is activism. We want the kingdom to come among us, but we forget that the kingdom of love has given us rebirth and with rebirth an astounding power: it has made us priests (Rev 1:6). The seal of the gift of the Spirit at our chrismation has given us a share in the priestly energy of Christ, who is servant of the Father and of mankind. Now the place where we need to be priests is in the liturgy that we live "among" men. The divine communion is captive in our societies, just as the divine beauty is in our cultures, and the agency that will set them free is our priesthood, which draws its vitality from the Holy Spirit. Love is "utopian": it is nowhere in our world, and no technique can produce it. Our spiritual priesthood is the power that effects its coming here and now. Certainties of this kind elicit a smile from activists, just as the eucharistic epiclesis does. In the judgment of carnal man nothing at all happens in the eucharistic epiclesis, and yet at that moment the entire world is penetrated by the divine communion and thereby survives and has life.

Just as in the sacramental epiclesis the world is present and is even offered to the loving desire of our Father so that his Spirit may incorporate it into the body of his Son, so too each ecclesial community in its lived epiclesis offers to the Father the social body to which it belongs according to the flesh. When the Spirit is thus petitioned, he comes down, penetrates the disfigured icon, and transfigures it in the communion of Christ. That is how the Church in every place lives out its saving priesthood through its members.

But this epicletic life of the Church in all our human groups is not something that occurs spontaneously. There must first be the realism of our sacramental celebrations; then the realism of the prayer of the heart; and, finally, the realism of communion in the Church. As a matter of fact, our ecclesial sense undergoes its severest test in our integration into society. Only there, as the days pass, can we experience wounded solidarity, the desperate longing for communion, the lack of love—in short, the weight of sin and death that lies heavy upon our human groups. Men must be reborn to love before they can feel its absence and offer this absence to him who longs to replace it with love's presence. Only "ecclesial souls" are capable of continual epiclesis, because their Lord brings them into his mystery as servant and priest, the mystery of the Lamb who carries and takes away the sin of the world. The source from which the river of life streams out is always the crucified and risen Lamb.

"We Have a Share in Each Other's Life" (1 Jn 1:7)

But the river of life renders fruitful the trees of life, whose very leaves are already "the cure for the nations" (Rev 22:2). The lived liturgy finds expression in "something active and genuine" (1 Jn 3:18).

If we are to be heedful above all of the prophetic and priestly aspects of the kingdom of the divine communion that exist in the midst of men, this is not in order that we may flee the present world. It is rather in order that we may avoid aping this world's death-dealing actions and instead bring forth the fruits of life. The third energy of the Holy Spirit has precisely this realistic purpose: to share with others the communion that causes us to exist as the Church.

For communion is indeed possible in our hopeless world; charity is no longer utopian; community among men is no longer beyond reach. The Church anticipates this communion by enabling us to share in the banquet of the kingdom. Now that the incorruptible body of Christ, who conquered death by love, has through us gained entry into our human groups, what will the result be? An entirely new inventiveness, a creativity reflective of grace and freedom, that must attack the absence of love at its very root or else go astray in an aesthetic charity. The radicalism of this communion manifests itself by humbly but resolutely reversing the relations that control our society, so as to focus society no longer on the mortal "ego" but on the mystery of the other. This life-giving un-self-centeredness that is at the source of the divine agape streams out into the world in the kenosis of the beloved Son and that of the Holy Spirit.

At the level of direct personal relationships, the finest parable of divine un-self-centeredness is perhaps that of the Good Samaritan. In the figure of this stranger, the unrecognized and despised neighbor, Jesus gives us an image of what we sinners imagine God to be (a distant, alien being who is our rival) and what we imagine the human person to be (the Incarnation scandalizes us to the extent that we have contempt for the human person). And yet this "Samaritan" God draws near to me, a man, a half-dead "Jew": this Other takes me on his back, becomes my neighbor, restores me to life. We must learn to see through the mute and bewildered eyes of the injured man of the parable. To do this, we must contemplate Jesus at length and enter humbly into the silence of his holy Name. It is in the liturgy of the heart that we learn how to become neighbors to our wounded fellow man; then the Holy Spirit will heal the relationship by making himself, the anointing of the New Covenant, a part of it. Whenever Christians consent to share in the kenosis of love of the Word and the Holy Spirit, communion is extended; a communion open to the kingdom can come into existence.

At the level of less directly personal relationships, that is, relations between groups, the fruit of communion turns out, if we reflect on it enough, to be the very object of the promise that was given to Abraham and fulfilled in Christ. The world of Babel is the world of the "nations" that rise up periodically against one another, a world of injustice, hatred, and death. In contrast, the seed of love that was offered to Abraham, accepted by him in faith, and made fruitful through obedience, is the seed of a "people" that is to be born not of flesh and blood or of the human will, but of God. It is in this people that justice and peace are to dwell. This people is born in Christ Jesus, a posterity according to faith and not according to the flesh. God alone knows who his people are amid the human ocean of the nations. But when this people acknowledge their God in his Son, they become the body of Christ. The Church is this body: a body always crucified, in which hatred is put to death, but also already risen, so that from her the Holy Spirit is poured out on all flesh. The service of communion that is entrusted to the Church is to turn a humanity made up of the "nations" into a humanity that is the "people of God". The Spirit of the promise dwells in the Church and causes her to move patiently toward the day when all men will be "his people, and he will be their God, God-with-them". On that day, "there will be . . . no more mourning or sadness or pain. The world of the past has gone" (Rev 21:3–4).

Chapter 19

Compassion, the Liturgy of the Poor

The wonder of the lived liturgy, then, is that in it the mystery of divine love becomes coextensive with our life. In its source, in its flow, in its fruits, this love seeks to permeate everything: the depths of the heart and of the person's being, work and culture, relations between individuals and the very texture of our societies. In this love the kingdom is already present and is coming "with power": the power of the crucified and risen Lord. But this same love also urges us to go ceaselessly further, as far as love can go (see Jn 13:1). The lived liturgy acquires its full realism and truth when it inspires us to enter into the depths of the world of sin, where love is not yet the conqueror of death. Philanthropy may be moral; charity is "mystical" because it reaches down in man to the abyss of death from which love is absent. The epiclesis of divine charity always takes place in its kenosis. Once we have been apprehended by it in our sacramental celebrations, how are we to live it out? The kenosis of love is revealed to us in the Bible as a mystery of poverty; if we consent to surrender to it, we will be able to experience and live the Church in her most divine and yet most human liturgy: the liturgy of compassion.

The Altar of the Poor

Poverty is a mystery. It is not to be gauged from outside, in the person of others; it is known in silence by those whom it burdens. And even if we experience its wounds, we are hardly able to give it a life-giving meaning, because it is an absence. Poverty cannot be objectified. Only he who incarnates it can reveal its mystery to us by giving us a share in it. Jesus is the Poor Man. He is more than a model of poverty; he is in his person the mystery of poverty. Jesus is our God, but God is the only being who has nothing. He does not have even a name, except for the name that we give him but that does not capture his being. He is; his name is "beyond everything".[1] In his person as the Son Jesus reveals to us that God is poor; for Jesus "has" nothing; he receives everything "from" the Father; he "is toward" the Father (*pros*: Jn 1:1–2).

When the Word espouses our flesh, he becomes poor in our humanity: poor with the poverty native to man who is made in the image of God and poor with the poverty of sinners who lack the glory of God. In Jesus the poverty of light and the poverty of darkness are assumed into his person, but in putting on the poverty of sin he restores the poverty of love. Jesus is "toward us" and gives us the One—the Holy Spirit—who proceeds from the Father and reposes in him. The Spirit of Jesus is "the Father of the poor". As a transparent presence he is not limited to any one place; as the "treasure house of all blessings" he is "everywhere present and fills everything".[2] Unlike the "prince of this world", the spirit of darkness who reveals himself in violence, the Holy Spirit is poor; that is why, without exercising constraint but in full freedom, he unites himself to man in his synergy. The fontal liturgy then becomes possible, because in it is accomplished the unlimited kenosis of love.

---

[1] Saint Gregory of Nazianzus.
[2] Opening invocation to the Holy Spirit in the Byzantine liturgy.

In the final analysis, poverty does not exist; only poor persons exist. If we serve the poor impersonally, we still connive with those who depersonalize them. The evil rich man of the parable is anonymous, like the death that disfigures man; the poor man of the parable is a person with a name: Lazarus, because when all is said and done this poor man is Jesus. He is Jesus not by a juridical pretense or by a pious shift of focus that unites us to Christ without real reference to the poor, but because of the shattering realism of the Incarnation of the poor Son: in him God becomes poor, so that henceforth the poor are God. "What you did to the least of these little ones . . .": the final judgment on all of our human behavior is based on the identity of Jesus and this poor person. The suffering of each man is the suffering of Jesus, who makes it his own. It is because of this mystical realism that each man is saved by Christ. Our death is no longer ours but his who died and rose for us. If Jesus were simply a model of poverty, we would still be prisoners of our death. He would not be the Good Samaritan who takes the human race on his back and pours out his life-giving Spirit upon it.

Did Mary, Martha's sister, have an insight into this mystery at Bethany, six days before the Passover, when she poured her precious ointment on the Lord? Be that as it may, when Jesus expressly asked that her gesture be included in the proclamation of the Gospel, he did so because it reveals an essential aspect of the good news: by acts of love we must continually save from death the very body that would soon be buried in our death. In his kenosis the Son of God made his own the suffering of every poor person; conversely, through love he suffers mysteriously in every man—for is there any man who is not poor—until "he has destroyed the veil which used to veil all peoples" and "has destroyed death for ever"? (Is 25:7–8). This is what Jesus means when he says, "You have the poor with you always" (Mk 14:7), just as "I am with you always; yes, to the end of time" (Mt 28:20). Because Christ in his body really passed through death and destroyed it, he can now incorporate into himself those who are still enslaved to death. The kingdom of God is in our midst because the body of Christ is still with us in this way. Love can spread abroad because the kenosis from which it streams forth is the death in which he was buried with us and for us.

When Saint John Chrysostom was trying to help the faithful of Antioch understand the mysterious unity between the liturgy they were celebrating and the liturgy they were to live out after leaving the church, he told them they were leaving the altar of the Eucharist only to go to the altar of the poor. The symbol used to express continuity is significant. We must now serve, in the persons of the poor, the same body of Christ that we served in the memorial of his Passion and Resurrection. At the celebration the altar was the sign of the tomb, the nonplace of death, and the origin of the new space of the Resurrection; in daily life the poor are the sign of the risen Christ from whom life-giving love can come.

The altar is also the symbol of the banquet table and the divine hospitality, which all men are invited to share. In the Eucharist we receive everything by sharing in the Body and Blood of Christ; at the altar of the poor we must respond by sharing the Gift we have received and by giving ourselves. We can understand why Andrei Rublev was always loath to paint a fresco of the Last Judgment in the apocryphal style so popular in the Middle Ages. He was too deeply in touch with the wretchedness of man to falsify in this way the mercy of his Lord. We all know what the fruit of Rublev's long silent fast was: the icon of the divine hospitality in which the altar of the world is received into the midst of the Blessed

Trinity. It is on the altar of the poor that the passion of God becomes the compassion of his Church for man.

The Church of Compassion

The hour of Jesus, in which he hands himself over with a love carried to the utmost, is henceforth the hour of the Church and our own hour. This hour is present for us in our lived liturgy each time that we draw near—become "neighbors" in the decentering of divine agape—to the poor who are our brothers. To be close to others does not mean being "like them" externally; when the beloved Son took flesh he did not mime our human ways but wedded himself to our poverty. The Church can serve the poor only by becoming poor like her Lord. But knowledge of the divine compassion for men is constantly made available to us, for it is revealed to each of us in the depths of our wretchedness. If we accept this wretchedness, we become "poor according to the Spirit"; at this point we achieve the transparency that makes possible a communion with the poor.

Knowledge of the divine compassion results from what is perhaps the most intense movement of the Spirit in our hearts. The Virgin Mary—who is the Church as she dawns in a single person—is the mirror of this knowledge, its vital space. To know this compassion from within requires more than self-acceptance in joyless resignation; it requires that we say "Yes" with our whole being to the love that gives us life; it requires that we accept ourselves from the hand of the Father and entrust the burden of our human nature to Jesus, who carries it for us. Once we have been re-created in mercy after having been created by necessity, we become free and are able to love; we become free, not in order to suffer more but in order that all suffering may be opened up like an unsealed spring. Let us learn to make our own the gaze of the Virgin of Tender Love, this searching gaze that sees afar because it comes from afar: from the heart of God himself. Our existence as part of the Church then becomes a burning bush that man cannot approach without hearing in his heart the same words that Moses heard: "I have indeed seen the misery of my people. . . . I have heard them crying for help. . . . I am well aware of their sufferings" (Ex 3:7). Our God is a Savior, but not one who stands far off. If no one can see him without experiencing death, how shall our brothers see him unless we "experience" their death?

Compassion streams forth like the river of life at the heart of the new Jerusalem, that is, of the Church that we ourselves comprise: "Look, I am going to send peace flowing over her like a river" (Is 66:12). Compassion wells up not from our feelings but from our hearts. Its first movement is creative forgiveness. This we learn within ourselves because we can be continually forgiven, without forcing ourselves to be sinners. We learn it above all in compassion itself, since if others do evil it is because they are first afflicted by evil. When we "know" or "experience" the death from which they suffer, our defensive fears disappear, and our aggressiveness falls away.

But peace-giving mercy is limitless; the divine compassion goes much further than simply forgiveness. It is obvious that our God forgives us sinners, for he is well aware of the dust from which we are made; then, too, his beloved Son has taken our flesh, and "can anything cut us off from the love of Christ?" (Rom 8:35). But there is in addition a real scandal, a stumbling block: the innocent suffer; the poor are oppressed; children are slaughtered. It is here that abyss of the divine compassion reveals itself.

We are once again at the heart of the epiclesis, where Job utters his cry and the groans of the poor arise from "underneath the altar" of the eternal liturgy (Rev 6:9ff.). The altar of burned sacrifice has become the altar of the poor and the altar of compassion. It is there that the Church experiences the hour of her lived liturgy, experiences it as the presence of love at the heart of the most profound absence. "Where are you, Lord? How long will you delay?" The Cross of his Son is the place from which he seems most absent but in which he in fact gives himself most completely. The place where his Christ is crucified is the place where his compassion is poured out, for it is the place where man is most deeply wounded by death. People today are surprised at the deep silence of God, probably because the power of death has thrown aside its mask; but who is willing to enter into the silence of the compassion of Jesus, to follow him that far? It is only a stone's throw between the slumber of the disciples and the agony of their Lord: to cross that space is to enter into the struggle of prayer, intercession, and compassion.

When we enter thus into the depths of the Name of the holy Lord Jesus, our whole being is in a state of epiclesis, and the Spirit Comforter pours himself out through us into the hearts of our suffering brothers. How does the Father of the Poor make himself a Comforter? Certainly not with empty words and barren emotions as we do! He who is the silence of the Word and the power at work in his Resurrection restores to the hearts of the poor the power to live and the joy that no one can take away. He possesses the secret of that compassion by which the poor in turn become an altar of salvation for their brothers. For to suffer with, to be powerless, is to share in the weakness of God on the Cross. We must believe and enter into this kenosis of the Word and his Spirit, into this kenosis of the Church that becomes ours through compassion. Without it there is no communion or community, no Resurrection or liberation. Instead of bemoaning the sufferings inflicted on us by others, let us learn to suffer with them; the "groaning of the Spirit" in them and in us will become a spring of life.

"The glory of God is man fully alive", says Saint Irenaeus; his radiant love makes men live. The most revealing manifestation of the glory of the Blessed Trinity is its mercy. When we allow ourselves to be apprehended by it, we enter into the depths of the heart of our God. But this glory that pours itself out in mercy is buried in the opaqueness of our death; it is hidden, during our last times, in the distress of the poor, just as it was, during the hour of the Cross, in the "man of sorrows, familiar with suffering, one from whom, as it were, we averted our gaze, [one] despised, for whom we had no regard" (Is 53:3). The glory of God is in a state of kenosis in man, and for that reason, though the final words of the Word are words of mercy, his final Breath is compassion. Since that moment, upon "the inhabitants of Jerusalem" there has been poured out "a spirit of grace and prayer, and they will look to ... the one whom they have pierced" (Zech 12:10; Jn 19:37). It is thus that the Spirit Comforter teaches us to look upon suffering man. "When that day comes"—and it has come for us—"a fountain will be opened for ... the inhabitants of Jerusalem" (Zech 13:1; Jn 19:34). Then the fontal liturgy becomes life giving: compassion is the liturgy of the poor.

Chapter 20

Mission and the Liturgy of the Last Times

We can reflect endlessly on theology and on the pastoral implementation of the Church's mission, but the mystery of this mission will become part of our lives only if our hearts are converted, tilled, and watered by the divine compassion. This compassion must make its dwelling in us. The lived liturgy begins its life-giving work in our hearts through more and more continuous prayer; with the heart at its starting point it then permeates our nature, our activity, and all our relationships. The more it divinizes us, the more our lives become God's work; the more the divine communion renews our relationships, the more we become the Church. The liturgy thus expands the Church into a human space for the divine compassion. It is at this moment of full growth that the mystery of the liturgy both celebrated and lived rends the heart of the Church, just as love rends the heart of the Father, and the Spirit rends the heart of Christ dying on the Cross. Then compassion streams out over the world, and behold, mission!

Before questioning anything, let us locate ourselves in the mystery; before posing problems let us learn to contemplate. Truly fruitful questions about mission make themselves known—and are answered—in the unity of the mystery. These fruitful questions are not formulated by opposing or preferring liturgy to mission; such an opposition or preference is utterly meaningless. Nor are they reached by juxtaposing the two, as though there were question of two specializations—one internal, the other external—in the Church.

Even though we can in fact distinguish between liturgical celebration and mission in the lived history of the Churches, the questions that arise concern first and foremost how we combine the two. Why is it, on the one hand, that the vitality of God's people, which is identifiable with the liturgy, does not express itself, or expresses itself so little, in mission, which is the fruit of charity? Why, on the other hand, do Christians invest so much generosity and ingenuity in things that are marginal to the liturgy and the essential mission of the Church? These it seems are the two preliminary questions that must be asked today. Other questions regarding the "how" of the mission are only corollaries, and their answer requires that we go back to the basic questions.

The source of the liturgy, namely, the living water that slakes the thirst of the baptized, awakens the thirst of the scattered sons of God. The same Spirit ensouls the "people of God" and groans in the heart of the "nations". In an earlier chapter, we contemplated in the liturgy of the last times three great synergies of the Spirit and the Church: that which reveals Christ, that which transforms everything into his body, and that which extends his communion.[1] We found these three, distinct but inseparable, present throughout the liturgy, both celebrated and lived. Now, it is these same three that inspire from within the entire movement of mission, as we shall see. When the river of life produces the fruit for the sake of which it streams forth from the Father and the Lamb (this production of fruit is its mission), it is always carried along by the same currents. The Church is not different when

[1] See chap. 8.

she celebrates the liturgy and when her members live out the liturgy; she simply exists differently. So too in her mission. She does not have one face turned toward God and another turned toward man. Her mission in the last times is to be both the human face of God, the face in which man can recognize him whom he is seeking, and, in the same light, the face of man, in which the glory of God is reflected (see 2 Cor 4:6).

The Paschal Mystery of Mission

It is in celebrating the eternal liturgy that the Church receives and learns her mission. The first men sent, the apostles par excellence, experienced it and wrote of it in the Acts of the Apostles. Today the Spirit imprints the meaning of the mission in the flesh of the Church. He is the one wholly Given, the one whom Jesus constantly sends, and he draws with him into the kenosis of his mission the living body of him who is the first emissary of the Father. The Spirit is at work in the hearts of all men, his base of operations being the center—the Church—where the overflowing compassion of the Father and the Son streams forth.

The mission of the Church is understandable only within the mystery of the last times. It is the final period of the economy of salvation in the present world. It is the power of the risen Lord drawing all men to the Father through the compassion of his Spirit, whom he pours out upon them. The mystery of the Ascension is the divine momentum that carries our world along. This omnipotent Ascension, wherein the divine liturgy began, is constantly wresting men from the sway of darkness and bringing them into the light of the Father. What is accomplished sacramentally in the celebrated liturgy is then unfolded in the mission as the integral liturgy of the Church. The one paschal mystery is received in its fullness in the celebrated liturgy and poured out in abundance in the mission. In one and the same passage the Church is transfigured in her Lord and also radiates the light of his life-giving body. The celebrated liturgy and the liturgy of mission are two phases of a single love. How can we love our brothers if we do not first welcome him who has loved us first? These are two movements within the one paschal mystery: "You are . . . a kingdom of priests . . . to sing the praises of God who called you out of the darkness into his wonderful light" (1 Pet 2:9).

A liturgical celebration is certainly a moment of intensity in which each ecclesial community renews its consciousness of its mission. Even more importantly, however, it is the moment in which the community's mission is given to it, not as a set of orders but in the very mystery of that mission. For it is here that the Word entrusts himself to his Church as a treasure in earthen vessels (2 Cor 4:7), by placing his word in its heart, filling it with his Spirit, handing over his body to it. Then the Church is able to tell all men of that which she holds engraved within her, to give them the Spirit by giving her own life, and to be the kingdom in their midst.

The great work of Christ's own passage becomes, in mission, the work of the Church. Is that not the deeper meaning of "liturgy" as action, vitality, divine work of the people of God? In the liturgical celebration the people of God becomes more and more the body of Christ; what does it do in its mission but make Christ become increasingly all in all? Above all, however, the liturgy teaches the people of God—and teaches them by doing—the one, unalterable meaning of that "missionary activity" "for us men and for our salvation" that is accomplished in the same dynamic movement as "the praise of the glory of his grace". A failing grasp of the doxological meaning of mission often goes hand in hand with a failing grasp of the divine meaning of human salvation. In Jesus these two distinct but inseparable finalities are united in the person of the Word and polarized by their common source of light, which is the Father. "The glory of God is man fully alive, and the life of man is the vision of God . . . for the glory of man is God, but the receptacle of the Energy of God and of his entire Wisdom and his entire Power is man." [2] The one, unchanged glory of God, which the Word came to restore by assuming and divinizing human nature— that is the paschal dynamic at work in the mission of the Church.

We learn to live this passage that is mission by "accomplishing" it in the celebration of the liturgy. This happens above all when the sacramental synergy carries us along in the anamnesis and epiclesis that are at the heart of the eucharistic anaphora. Here men are reached in the very state in which they await salvation—and this is precisely the criterion that distinguishes authentic expressions of mission. In the liturgy we find men at the place where God meets them and Christ makes himself the servant of mankind. During his mortal life Jesus supplied no social services, not even when he multiplied the loaves. His service is divine and is accomplished in liturgy and mission, by saving men in the place where, hungry, thirsty, and wounded by death, they are looking for God.

Christ, the servant of man for man's salvation, teaches us the same detachment from self in the liturgical celebration as in mission. From a social viewpoint the service of the one liturgy is useless; it changes no structures. But humanly, at

[2] Saint Irenaeus, *Against the Heresies* IV, 20, 7; III, 20, 2.

the level of essential human truth, it is the highest form of service, the service of divinizing compassion. In the liturgical celebration we live out the passage of man in Christ, the same passage at whose service we are in mission. Once we have realized that the eucharistic epiclesis is the source of that compassion from which all the energies of the Church flow, we will be able to understand how mission manifests and communicates the divine compassion that saves men.

Mission, Epiphany of Compassion

In the eucharistic anaphora the passage of Jesus for all men becomes ours. But if some of his members rejoice at passing into life, how can they not suffer at the same time for those who are still in death? In the liturgy of the word Christ the Savior is revealed to us, and we respond with an acceptance inspired by faith. But our response would be a betrayal of him who entrusts himself to us if we did not then proclaim him. The mission is this manifestation of Christ to the world by everything that we are: ecclesial community, word, witness, gift of our lives.

Mission in its primary meaning is essentially an epiphany of Christ through his Church as the new community of love. The Church is not a worldwide production line for publicizing the Gospel or an association of branch groups to which the disciples of Jesus belong; she is the newness of the communion of the Holy Spirit present among men. The good news that she proclaims by her mere existence is that impossible love is here as a real event. The living God does not put in an appearance: he is, and he is coming. The same holds for the Church as event of divine love among men. If the Church does not become herself by receiving the Holy Spirit, who turns her into the body of Christ, she is nothing more than one sociocultural group among others; it is then that, lacking the fontal liturgy, Christians fall back on publicity. But if the local Church is a community of charity, men may reject this overwhelming news of God's love for them, but they cannot fail to see it. Mission as epiphany means first of all this mystery of light (Jn 13:35).

With this as its point of departure, mission is also the coming of the word. Through baptism and chrismation each member of the Church receives charisms for the new kind of prophecy that consists in "completing the coming of the word of God" (Col 1:25) among men. The word "completes its mission" (2 Thess 3:1) provided we proclaim it as it truly is and without adulterating it (2 Thess 2:3; 2 Cor 2:17): provided, that is, we proclaim Jesus crucified and risen. To the extent that we allow him to shine through us, he calls men where they are, that is, still in darkness, and leads them from light to light.

Because he, only Friend of man, understands him, he is able to lay hold of him and set him free. Jesus is neither demagogue nor dogmatician; he is the pure light of the Father's glory. He speaks through us "with authority" and not as a commentator; the truth of what he says reflects what is, and simple, upright hearts are able to see this. He is the only truly human being, because he knows in his own flesh both the struggle sinners have and the freedom to live divinely as a man. That is why our words, which are the sacrament of his mystery, are neither discourse about God nor moral code for man, but the revelation that these men are loved and called to become God because the Father has first loved them and because his Son has become one of them. The word we proclaim will be all the truer to the extent that it has first transformed us by divinizing us.

If the Church is to proclaim the Gospel through us, our whole being must be engaged in the work. Mission cannot but take the form of witness. Jesus is the unparalleled witness to the Father's tender love and the wretchedness of man. He is also the faithful witness, because he fulfills in himself the promise the Father has given to all of his children; I mean that the divine greatness is now restored in the beloved Son. John was the finger pointing to the Word in the lowliness of his flesh. The Church, which exists in the Holy Spirit and shares in his kenosis, is now the precursor of the Lord on the threshold of his coming in glory. But it does not manifest Christ as one who stands outside it; John was the friend of the Bridegroom; the Church is the Bride. The mystery of witness, which is too often reduced to outward manifestations, demands an awesome degree of transparency. Witness is not something that can be improvised. It requires a long intimacy with the Word of life and with the death of the man toward whom it draws us; it requires a compassion that is always new, like that of the Virgin Mary.

Finally, the mission of the word reaches its completion in martyrdom, the supreme form of witness. The form that the martyrdom takes is unimportant; the important thing is that the mission of the Church would no longer be the mission of Christ and the Holy Spirit if it did not reach this climax. "What does it matter to you? You are to follow me" (Jn 21:22). We can be witnesses of him whom we have heard, whom our eyes have seen and our hands have touched, only if his fire purifies us until we are wholly conformed to him. From the epiclesis of our baptism to the epiclesis of our Eucharists, the same fire is at work in us in order that Life may do its work in our brothers. If our mission does not encounter opposition, we are false prophets. Though we are sent to be with men, we cannot be like them; we can truly

be with and for them only if we are, like Christ, "a sign that
is opposed" (Lk 2:34) and that reveals the secrets of hearts.
Tribulation—suffered because we are "Christ-ians" (1 Pet
4:16)—is the seal upon the ministry of the word, its completion in the silence of the love that gives life after having
first given the "imperishable seed" of life (1 Pet 1:23). The
mission begun in the liturgy of the Church is thus brought
to completion in the eternal liturgy. In martyrdom compassion reaches the utmost limits of love.

Mission, Pentecost of the Last Times

The mission of the Church is not intermittent, any more
than the love of the Father for each man is intermittent.
But we cannot always be proclaiming him whom we contemplate or always helping our brothers to achieve freedom
in the Holy Spirit. What then are we to do, since we cannot
at every moment be breaking the bread for which man
hungers and pouring out the oil that heals all his wounds?
Some turn back to their nets. Others are too filled with the
compassion of their Lord to leave the Church alone in the
time of her confinement; after all, is she not carrying him
who is becoming all in all? Mission thus turns back to its
wellspring, lest it lose its vitality; it is the prayer of the heart
that ensures the liturgy of mission will never become a
dried-up stream.

In the epiclesis of the Eucharist our prophetic and kingly
priesthood, a priesthood of word and love, draws strength
from a fire that is never extinguished. The liturgy of the heart
always finds glowing embers there, and prayer is rekindled in
the vigor and fire of the epiclesis. The prayer of the heart,
which is in hidden communion with the groans of the saints

underneath the altar of the eternal liturgy, is the place where the Spirit constantly pours himself out upon men. In this unbroken Pentecost of the last times, the Holy Spirit is "the place of the saints", as Saint Basil puts it.[3]

So it also was at the very dawn of the fullness of time. This mystery of outpouring, which is the mission of the Spirit, began for him with the Virgin Mary. No sooner had she conceived the Word of the Father than she left "in great haste" for the home of her cousin Elizabeth, where in wishing peace she also gave it: the Spirit entered into the mother, and her child already experienced the vibrations of the Paraclete. Even when the Church is useless as far as the world is concerned, it is always on its mission, engaged in the "visitation" of men. The prayer that fills the heart of the Church is the epiclesis of its unbroken mission.

Constant prayer of this kind is a gift included in the Seal of the Gift of the Spirit, who has "confirmed" our baptism. When it is manifested through a personal call and lays hold of the entire being and life of an individual, it becomes the charism that will never have a truly satisfactory canonical name in the Church: the charism of monastic life. This is the virginal charism of the Church. Those clad in it hand over to the Holy Spirit, the Lord of the impossible, everything in the human person who normally looks to other men for his fulfillment: will, power, possession. This looking to the Holy Spirit for everything is the first movement of the epiclesis, of the prayer of the heart. Monastic life is thus a hidden charism, but its hiding place is in the front lines of the eschatological combat, and it supports the entire mission of the Church. In the words of Saint Thérèse of the Child Jesus, to live a monastic life is to be love at the heart of the Church.

---

[3] Saint Basil, *Treatise on the Holy Spirit* (PG 26:184A).

There is an icon in the Eastern Churches that is beginning to be rediscovered by their sisters in the West and that very accurately expresses this mystery of the Church at prayer on the Pentecost of the last times. It is the icon known as the *Deisis*.[4] At its center Christ holds the scroll of history (the crucified and risen Lamb) in one hand and with the other blesses the world (outpouring of the Holy Spirit); it is always in his Ascension that the mystery of mission is revealed and accomplished. On either side, the Virgin Mary and John the Baptist, their hands open and outstretched, are in a state of pure prayer, intercession, the groaning of the Spirit. Mary is always there as Church of the visitation of God in the midst of humanity; but he whom she once carried and who was filled with the Holy Spirit is now in the eternal liturgy. "Blessed are you who have believed" (Lk 1:45) is the Beatitude of the Church, for her compassion cannot fail to bear an eternal fruit.

[4] Literally "prayer, petition".

The Liturgy, Handing on of the Mystery

Mission is not something we must invent for ourselves. It is given to us, and we must carry it out, "celebrate" it. By going back to its source we have found, if we needed to, that neither does the liturgy have to be reinvented; it is for us to enter into it and be carried along by its life-giving stream.

We are in the presence here of the wonder of the mystery of Christ: from the beginning of creation to the full establishment of the kingdom, that mystery is handed on. Holy, living tradition, divine "tradition", is, when all is said and done, the passionate love of the Father, who "surrenders" his Word and "pours out" his Breath even to the point of "this is my body, *given up* for you; this is my blood, *shed* for you" and "Jesus *gave up* his spirit". The passionate love of the Father for man (see Jn 3:16) reaches its climax in the Passion of his Son and is thenceforth poured out by his Spirit in the divine compassion at the heart of the world, that is, in the Church. And the mystery of tradition is this joint mission of the Word and the Spirit throughout the economy of salvation; now, in the last times, all the torrents of love that pour from the Spirit of Jesus flow together in the great river of life that is the liturgy.

In the economy of salvation tradition first took the form of the gift of saving events; in the liturgy it fulfills and renders present the event that sustains all of history: the Passage of Jesus, but it does so with the Church, and this is the central synergy of the epiclesis. In the economy of salvation tradition next showed itself as the revelation of the meaning of the saving events by the prophets and sacred writers; in the liturgy it manifests Christ to the Church and through the Church, and this is the synergy of the memorial. In the economy of salvation tradition was, finally, the participation of the people of God in the saving events; in the liturgy, it is the synergy of communion, in which celebration and life are henceforth inseparable. The channels of divine tradition are those of the "varied graces of God" (1 Pet 4:11), but the living water is always the water of the river "rising from the throne of God and the Lamb and flowing crystal clear".

The liturgy is the great river into which all the energies and manifestations of the mystery flow together, ever since the very body of the Lord who lives with the Father has been ceaselessly "given up" to men in the Church in order that they may have life. The liturgy is not something static, or a mental memorial, a model, a principle of action, a form of self-expression, or an escape into angelism. It reaches far beyond the signs in which it manifests itself and the effectiveness it contains. It is not reducible to its celebrations, although it is indivisibly contained in them. It finds expression in the human words of God that are written in the Bible and sung by the Church, but these never exhaust it. It is at home in all cultures and not reducible to any of them. It unites the multitude of local Churches without causing them to lose their originality. It feeds all the children of God, and it is in them that it ceaselessly grows. Although it is constantly being celebrated, it is never repeated but is always new.

If we have entered into the vision of John as he contemplates at the heart of history the onward sweep of the river of life that is the liturgy, all the ways in which we separate celebration and life have been pushed aside and left behind. This omnipotent attraction of the Christ of the Ascension is now inscribed in the depths of every human event and is able to illumine it from within and communicate life there. We cannot reduce it to a few flashes of communion or to festive moments of communal celebration. The total Christ event that is the liturgy and in which we are constantly involved extends far beyond the consciousness of faith and the celebrations of believers. It assumes and permeates all of history, as well as all men and each of them in all their dimensions, and the whole cosmos and all of creation. We desire to be carried along by this river: may this good fortune be ours now that we have reached its source.